GUIDE   PURPOSE   SECRET

For a Happier Marriage

What they should
have told me!

Rabbi Aaron Laine

ISBN 978-0-692-54396-2

Copyright © 2015 by Rabbi Aaron Laine

www.gpsmarriage.com
rabbilaine@gpsmarriage.com

Printed in the United States of America

To my dear wife
Fradel
a true *eshet chayil*

Acknowledgments

I WOULD LIKE TO thank those who, over the years, placed their trust in my marriage counseling—both members of my congregation as well as people from the extended Jewish community in Panama.

The board of our synagogue and women's auxiliary gave me their constant support, especially the former president, Bruce Eisenman, who suggested I take on this project. Thanks to Len Estrin for developing my ideas in the first draft, Mrs. Suri Brand who really did a superb job on redoing and finishing the work, Mrs. Bracha Steinberg for proofreading and giving it the final touches, and Mrs. Eden Chachamtzedek for the page layout and design.

I would also like to thank all those people who read my book and gave me invaluable feedback, especially the psychologists and professionals Robert Schwartz, Issac Shagalow, Lea Setton, Marci Mizrachi, and Patricia Bentolila. In addition, my appreciation to Moises Attias, Michael Bettsak, Jonathan Bettsak, Dorita Eisenman, Danny Nelkenbaum, my in-laws Ephraim and Toebe Potash, my dear mother Henya Laine, Michael and Yael Rubin, Danny and Lisa Yaker, and Bruce Zalcer.

Rabbis Manis Friedman, Moshe Rapaport, Avrohom Plotkin, Raphael Aron, and Shiye Rubinstein also deserve special mention.

A special thanks to Jaco and Greta Lacks, who supported this project financially and made this book a reality.

To my parents, Rabbi David and Henya Laine, who provided a caring and loving environment for me to grow up in and develop the talents G-d gave me.

To our children Mushkie, Mendel, and Shlomo, who bring us great joy and *nachat*.

To the Lubavitcher Rebbe, *zy'a*, for inspiring me by his example of how to dedicate one's life to helping others.

And without question, to the Source of everything, G-d Al-mighty, for all His blessings.

Rabbi Aaron Laine

Contents

Appendices

Introduction

A FAMOUS CELEBRITY IN Panama, where I serve as a rabbi, came to me for help. She shared with me the problems she was experiencing in her marriage, and I gave her some advice. As she turned to leave, I asked, "Why did you come to me? Didn't you consult your priest about this?"

"Of course I did," she replied.

"What did he say?"

"He said I should pray."

"And?"

"I prayed," she said. "The prayer didn't work, so I went back to the priest."

"What did he say then?"

"He said, 'Pray harder.' That didn't work either, so I came to you."

I nodded. "I imagine that giving advice about marriage can be quite a challenge for a person who has never been married!"

Shortly afterward, I had a visit from a synagogue member who was having marital troubles. I had given him advice, but his relationship remained a mess. "Rabbi, what do you suggest now?" he asked.

What could I say?

"Pray."

My wife and I moved to Panama over twenty years ago when the Ashkenazic community was looking for a rabbi. Six months after we arrived, a couple came to me for help. Their marriage was in trouble. I was eager to help them, but I was only twenty-five years old and had been married a mere eight months. What advice could I possibly give to a couple who had been married for fifteen years?

I realized quickly that I'd better get some experience in marriage counseling because this was going to be a part of my job. As I soon found out, in Panama most couples came to the rabbi when they had marriage problems before they even thought of seeing a psychologist. It was clear that I needed to hone my marriage counseling skills.

> Don't tell jokes about marriage. The women don't think they're funny and the men don't think they're jokes.

Over the next few years I took notes and began to develop some ideas of my own about what makes a marriage work and what doesn't. After about five years on the job, I compiled my notes in a booklet. By then I thought I had all the answers. I was confident that my ideas were accurate masterpieces of great advice. I thought that if I could publicize my theories, I could help many more couples.

Eager to get a confirmation of my theories, I asked two rabbis who were spiritual leaders of prominent congregations to give me their opinions, certain they would agree that these ideas could benefit countless couples. The first one was very polite, made a few corrections, and sent them back to me. The second told me frankly, "This is good for amateurs."

I was devastated. *How could he say that about such a novel approach? What does he know about marriage anyway?* I rationalized. I honestly thought that I was right on the money.

Over a decade later, I can say he was right — the ideas were good, but they weren't developed enough. I have been working as a community rabbi for almost two decades now. I have met with hundreds of couples. I've come to see a pattern over time, and I've noticed that most of the issues that are the source of their marital problems are similar, whether they've been married a short time or for many years. Analyzing the reasons for the problems, I've come to understand the source of these issues, and these findings have formed the basis for this book.

Happy Marriages = Healthy Communities

A HAPPY MARRIAGE BENEFITS not only the couple, but is vital for the entire community.

I believe that keeping families whole is fundamental to the welfare of society in general, and the Jewish people in particular. How can a community be considered good and healthy when people's marriages are falling apart and kids are growing up in broken homes?

People try to convince me that children raised by divorced parents are perfectly fine. And, yes, some have been able to overcome this trauma. Often, however, this is not the case. The effects of divorce can be devastating to the family and the community.[1]

When children are brought up in a home with both a father and mother, for instance, it's much easier to set limits. The parents can be united in their discipline and the child is much less likely to be able to pit one parent against the other. This gives the child a sense of security as he learns self-discipline.

When parents divorce, often each parent tries to get the children "on their side," and usually spoils them. The result is a child brought up without discipline or structure. The less structure the

---

1. Patrick Fagan, PhD, "The Effects of Divorce on Children," *Remarks to the World Congress of Families* II (November 8, 1999).

child has, the greater the tendency to look for other ways to feel secure and good about himself — usually ways that are not good for the child.

Discipline and self-control are fundamental for a healthy, functioning society. It's much harder for a person to become a healthy member of the community if he didn't grow up with a secure family structure.

This is just one example of the effects of divorce on society. I have spent years analyzing the nature of the marital relationship and why couples behave as they do and, in some cases, end up divorcing. I feel that if couples are more knowledgeable about the nature of the relationship, they will be better equipped to strengthen their marriage and prevent divorce. In this book I offer a tried-and-true method for a happy, healthy marriage and a happy, healthy community.

The Elusive Happy Marriage

SPEAKING AT A CONFERENCE in Cali, Colombia, a few years ago, I asked the audience, "How long does it take to become a lawyer?"

"Four years," someone said.

"A doctor with a specialty?"

"Ten years," was the reply.

"What is more difficult — being a lawyer, doctor, or a spouse?"

"A spouse," answered the overwhelming majority.

"How many years do we study about relationships before we marry?"

"Zero."

"This is absurd," I pointed out. "Wouldn't it make sense to learn how to succeed in marriage before actually marrying?"

Someone in the audience shouted, "Then for sure no one would get married!"

When I began researching the reasons that so many marriages are unhappy, I wondered: How is it possible that the institution of marriage has existed for thousands of years, and so many people still haven't figured out how to make it work? You would think that with all the latest advances in technology, medicine, and the sciences, we would have learned the secret to a happy marriage.

We have been able to discover how people with severe disabilities can communicate and manipulate objects using only their brainwaves. We have created new materials with properties alchemists could only dream of. People have flown aboard rockets to outer space — not as scientists, but as *tourists*. Yet we are no happier than people were a hundred years ago. The divorce rate is higher than ever, and even if a couple manages to remain married, often they are not happy in the relationship.[2]

Why haven't we been able to figure out how to make the most fundamental institution in society function smoothly?

It's not like people haven't tried. Acclaimed psychologists have addressed the challenge. They have produced tens of thousands of pages filled with ideas and advice on marriage. Yet some of them are divorced themselves or dissatisfied with their own relationships. People continue to publish new books on the topic. Many of those books make it to the best-seller lists as people desperately seek answers to their marriage problems.

If there's so much information out there, why are so many people still unhappy?

---

2. As of 2010, 20% of couples get divorced within five years, 32% of couples who are together ten years are getting divorced, and of those together twenty years, 48% — nearly half — end up divorced. See Casey E. Copen, PhD, et al., "First Marriages in the United States: Data from the 2006–2010 National Survey of Family Growth," *National Health Statistics Reports* 49 (March 22, 2012).

These are the questions I asked myself as I developed my own ideas about making marriage work.

When I thought about it, I realized the reason is obvious. A lot of people don't follow the advice given by these specialists. At the end of the day, a good, healthy marriage requires effort, dedication, and commitment. The lawyer and the doctor invest a lot of years and hard work in their careers. Does a marriage deserve any less?

It's hard to change. Breaking addictive habits like smoking is hard enough; it's even harder to change our nature, which is the cause of the bad habits. Yet it can, and must, be done. Before we can even get to the root of the problem, we must be committed to resolving it. In this book, we will go to the root of the problem that causes unhappy marriages. But I must warn you that if you have no interest in really working to make your marriage flourish, reading this book will be futile. If you are interested and up for the challenge, then read on!

The Smoke Screen

SUPPOSE YOU HAVE A child who is clever and intelligent, but he's not doing well in school. Naturally you're upset and you want to get him to improve. You form all types of theories as to why your child is failing. You question the child, but he can't put the problem into words. Perhaps you blame the child for his lack of effort and interest. If the problem persists, you might encourage your child to change, using either rewards or punishments. You might also accuse the teacher or the school of not addressing the issue. Somehow the problem isn't being resolved, and your frustration grows as conflict about the issue among the child's teachers and administrators escalates.

But what if the problem is that your kid needs glasses and no one realized it? Or he has a chronic hearing problem and has to read lips to understand what the teacher is saying? Or maybe he is dyslexic or hyperactive. Instantly, you would change your approach. You would address the cause instead of trying to control the symptoms.

In another common scenario, a father comes home from work tired and drained. His daughter acts sullen and obnoxious at the dinner table. His automatic reaction is to put her in her place. But often a teenager's surliness is a facade — a smoke screen. What the father needs to do is to uncover the real reason for her behavior. If he digs deep enough, he will find the answer: a falling-out with a friend, a failed test, a slight from a teacher. Then he can address the cause and the symptoms will disappear.

Let's take a look at some of the most common reasons people give to identify problems in their relationships:

We have a lack of communication: This expression is politically correct code for "Men have a difficult time communicating. They prefer to manage their problems alone and aren't accustomed to sharing their feelings." Or: "Women never tell men what's really bothering them. Instead, men get the silent treatment, and then they just end up fighting."

He/she has unrealistic expectations: Translated, this expression means, "When I married him, I expected him to be a real gentleman, that he would make me feel loved, cherished, and respected, but sometimes he is so insensitive and selfish — too focused on his work, too passionate about his hobbies, or too involved with his friends. I thought I would never be lonely when I married, but now I feel not only lonely, I feel neglected!" Or: "I thought my wife would take care of my needs just like my mother takes care of my father, while giving him space and not nagging him when he wants to go out and have coffee with his friends."

He/she is so demanding and complains all the time: Requests that range from mowing the lawn to helping kids with their homework to spending more quality time with each other suddenly turn into demands and complaints when the relationship sours.

After working with so many couples, I've come to realize that these grievances — and others like them — are a smokescreen for a core problem. If they would resolve the core problem, the symptoms would disappear.

When we focus on the core of the problem, we can eliminate the problem. This is precisely what this book is about: identifying the source of the problems in marriage and offering ways to resolve them.

The first chapters of this book focus on the importance of good self-esteem and the things people seek to feel good about themselves. Men and women have different needs and look for different things. We'll identify what those things are and understand why this is a reason couples start to drift away from each other.

The next chapters will focus on solutions and what you can do to change the dynamic so that your relationship will become stronger rather than fall apart in the face of these needs.

Finally, we'll focus on various techniques for avoiding conflict and resolving fights.

Below you will find real-life examples to illustrate some of the ideas. All names and places have been changed to protect people's privacy.

An Important Disclaimer

IT'S IMPORTANT TO NOTE that the suggestions for improving marriage in this book will work only if both spouses are emotionally stable — that is, they do not suffer from any type of emotional imbalance, trauma, or addiction. People who don't have serious issues or baggage also need to be taught the basics of how to maintain a good relationship. However, if one or both marital partners have an emotional imbalance (whether it's bipolar disorder, seasonal affective disorder, depression, or postpartum depression), in order to expect concrete results they must seek professional treatment. Relying on the advice in this or any self-help book will be a waste of time and energy and may even cause harm.

A person with an emotional imbalance can come across as very rational, and it's tempting to think that you can work things out on your own. But a mental or emotional imbalance is an illness. No matter how much you try to explain, convince, apologize, and clarify, the situation will not improve until you stop trying to reason with this person and go for qualified, professional help.

Likewise, if one spouse suffers from an addiction, it's important to seek professional help. An addiction can be fatal to a marriage and must be addressed before any marriage counseling will help.

PART 1

The P's and the A's

1 The Pursuit of Happiness

What Makes You Happy?

IF I ASKED YOU, "What are you looking for in life?" how would you respond? Do you desire money? Power? Health? Peace of mind? All of the above?

I've asked this question hundreds of times, and people give all types of answers. But no matter the response, it usually boils down to happiness. If you lack health or peace, this usually affects your happiness. If you can't pay the rent, grocery bill, or children's school tuition, this creates anxiety that doesn't permit you to be happy.

By nature or nurture, happiness is something we all seek. We all want to be happy. We can't stand to suffer anxiety, pain, sadness, loss, or anything else that makes us feel bad.

So how do we get happiness? Can we buy it in the mall? Does it have a price?

As absurd as it sounds, many people do believe that happiness can be purchased. They spend their money trying to obtain it, but they confuse momentary pleasure with true happiness. Eventually

> My wife and I were very happy. Then we met.

they become addicted to the rush they get from buying a new pair of sunglasses or a new car. When the rush is over, they need to do something else to bring it back. But at the end of the day, happiness isn't measured by how many things you can buy or what you've accomplished.

So where does it come from? Is there a secret formula?

It seems that some people are just born happy and the rest of us don't stand a chance. And, yes, people do exist who are naturally happier than others, just as there are optimists and pessimists, extroverts and introverts, sociable and unsociable people. Still, happiness is within everyone's reach. There are no guarantees, of course. But unless a person has a chemical imbalance or disorder that prevents him from feeling joy, every human being can be happy.

> The wise men of Chelm realized that people were wasting too much time worrying. They hired Moshe to be the town's official worrier. From now on, anyone who had a problem would take it to Moshe, and Moshe would worry about it for them.
>
> Moshe went home and told his wife the good news. "I've just been hired for a new job," he said. "It's steady work and it pays well."
>
> Chana was elated. "Moshe, that's wonderful!"
>
> "But I have a problem," Moshe added.
>
> "What's that?" she asked.
>
> "Now that I have a job, I have no worries."

Self-Esteem: The Road to Happiness

OUR SENSE OF SELF is shaped primarily by our childhood, upbringing, and family structure. We received these building-blocks of our self-esteem as children, and we need them to help us deal with life's challenges. Still, as adults, whether or not we had a strong, positive sense of self as children, we still seek things that make us feel good — things that boost our self-esteem.

> People who suffer from low self-esteem, unless they do something about it, are usually not upbeat and joyful.[1]
>
> Understandably, they suffer from what is popularly known as identity problems — feelings of worthlessness that are devastatingly depressing. It becomes evident that self-esteem is essential for *simchah* (happiness).

It is precisely the things that strengthen self-esteem, such as having a good marriage, a successful career, and a nice lifestyle, that produce long-term happiness. Conversely, things that do not strengthen self-esteem will never make us happy, no matter how much we have.

> Self-esteem and happiness are interdependent.[2]

Long-term happiness is built on a foundation of a strong, positive self-image. A person who is satisfied with who he is, what he has, and his accomplishments is a happy person.[3]

> People with a positive self-image are more likely to take chances, deepen relationships, learn, and grow. Those with low self-esteem, on the other hand, have trouble forming close, lasting relationships. They become paralyzed at the idea of trying new things and in severe circumstances even stop functioning altogether.

---

1. Rabbi Dr. Abraham Twerski, *Let Us Make Man: Self-Esteem through Jewishness* (CIS Publications, 1989), p. 42.

2. Twerski, *Let Us Make Man*, p. 103.

3. I am not saying that long-lasting true happiness comes from material success alone. I am convinced that a spiritual dimension with a sense of real purpose is very important, but this is beyond the scope of my book. Rabbi Twerski wrote, "Spiritual joy is dependent on a feeling that one is worthwhile, that one's life has a purpose and that there is significance to one's existence in the universe" (*Let Us Make Man*, p. 157).

If self-esteem is the basis of happiness, clearly our socio-economic class does not necessarily correspond to our level of happiness. People can be poor and happy, and they can be wealthy and miserable. It is how we view ourselves and our lives that determines our state of mind.

Ask yourself, "Am I happy with what I have or do I expect more from my life? My job, my family, my home, my status — do they fulfill my expectations or do I want to be someone else or somewhere else?" Whether it is material things like a luxury car or a spiritual accomplishment like peace of mind, what you view as valuable is the scale that measures your level of happiness.

The problem is that in today's society, we tend to judge our worth by other (and others') parameters. We look at someone else's job, family, house, car, health, status, or fame as a measure of our own. It's a natural tendency, but not a very productive one. Our self-esteem fluctuates depending on our feeling of achievement and success at the moment.

What it all boils down to is that happiness depends on your perception. In other words, your self-worth is established by your mindset, by how you view yourself and what you have. In turn, your self-worth contributes to your sense of well-being and happiness.

In Panama, there is a saying: "Money is not happiness. It's the step before happiness." We live in a material world and a great percentage of people believe that their self-worth is tied to their material worth. They believe that if only they had money, they would be happy. There's a story about a famous actor who had made it to the top and committed suicide. He left a suicide note, in which he wrote, "I thought if I made it to the top, I would be happy. But when I got there, there was nothing there." He thought that if he'd have fame, wealth, and everything money could buy he would be happy. When he had it all, he realized that it didn't really fulfill him. He still wasn't happy.

So when we say that we are pursuing happiness, what we are really saying is that we are looking for things that will boost our self-esteem. But since our self-esteem depends on our perception of our self-worth, if our self-worth is tied to our material possessions or physical accomplishments, then our happiness will hinge on what we have rather than who we are.[4]

> An immigrant from Russia was learning English. He asked an American friend, "What is the difference between a recession and a depression?"
>
> His friend replied, "A recession is when your business is doing badly. A depression is when *my* business is doing badly!"

The Key to Life

IT IS CLEAR FROM the Torah that self-esteem is a necessity for life. King Solomon compares marriage to goodness in one expression and death in another.[5]

How can he compare marriage to both extremes at the same time?

When our self-esteem is at its peak, which can be achieved by having a good marriage, we feel alive. All is well! When our

---

4. Why were we made this way? Wouldn't it be better if we would just be content with the way things are? Why do we have to have this need to pursue happiness?

G-d, in His wisdom, created human beings with the need to accomplish. If we had no need to produce, the world would not advance. People would not feel the need to invent and create; they would be satisfied with the simple things in life. The fact that we feel fulfilled when we create, achieve, acquire, and invent is necessary for the individual and the world.

5. In Proverbs 18:22, King Solomon teaches, "One who has found a wife has found goodness." In Ecclesiastes 7:26, he says, "I have discovered something that is more bitter than death: the wife…"

self-esteem is crushed, which happens occasionally in marriage, we are at the brink of death — perhaps not physically, but psychologically. Self-esteem is not a separate part of our life; it *is* our life.

We find this idea in the Talmud. The Talmud states, "A poor man is considered dead."[6] We can perhaps understand this on the literal level: When a person is poor, his self-esteem is more easily shattered and this can be compared to being dead. On a deeper level, the Talmud clarifies that wealth and poverty are all about one's perspective.[7] In Judaism, a person who is poor can be considered wealthy if he is satisfied with what he has.[8] In other words, it's not your material wealth that brings contentment, but rather your outlook as to what is important.

So if I have a healthy self-esteem, I am rich and alive no matter how many material possessions I actually have. And if I feel unfulfilled and I don't believe I am achieving my life's dream, I am a poor man and to an extent a dead man.

Anyone who has that feeling of dissatisfaction and chronic unhappiness has experienced that feeling of not really living. That's why I believe that a positive self-image is vital to a happy, healthy, vibrant life.

Everyone wants to be happy. To achieve happiness, we seek things that make us feel good and give us self-worth to feel happy.

---

6. Talmud, *Nedarim* 64b.
7. Talmud, *Nedarim* 41a.
8. See Mishnah, *Avot* 4:1.

2 Men and the Three P's

A COLLEAGUE OF MINE AND his wife went to lunch with a popular radio host. They were interrupted several times by people who recognized her. Every time, she would politely introduce my friend. "This is my rabbi and his wife," she'd tell them.

At the end of the meal, someone came over to the table, this time to greet the rabbi. Here, finally, was someone who knew the rabbi and not the famous radio host. "Let me introduce you to our friend," he said. "She's a well-known radio host!"

"That felt good!" the rabbi told me later when he recounted the story.

In the previous chapter, we established that self-esteem depends on what we decide is important to us. If we have the things we value, we feel good. Since happiness is so fundamental to our existence, we have a strong drive to pursue the things that make us happy. However, although everyone has a drive to pursue happiness, which results from having self-esteem, men and women pursue this in very different ways.

> A successful man is one who makes more money than his wife spends. A successful woman is one who finds such a man.

Before I tell you what they are, I'll begin with a disclaimer: There are exceptions to every rule. It's possible that a woman will possess the traits that are usually more common in men and vice versa. But in many cases and in my experience, there are certain traits common among men and certain traits common among women that we can identify and explore.

The Three P's

IF YOU ARE A man reading this, try this little exercise. Read the following questions or statements and record your thoughts:

- ⊕ What are the things that make you feel good?
- ⊕ What do you pursue with enthusiasm?
- ⊕ Describe the things that boost your self-esteem and make you feel fulfilled.

Some men might list "good health" as something that provides them with good self-esteem. People who are in poor health can find it difficult to feel good about themselves. In this exercise, however, we are not talking about basic needs; we are trying to determine what makes us feel good, assuming that our immediate needs — such as health, food, and shelter — are not an issue. So when you answer the questions above, leave aside essential basics that everyone needs for their well-being. List only those things that you seek after your immediate needs have been met. Here are some items that might appear on your list:

- ⊕ a good job;
- ⊕ intelligence;
- ⊕ good-looking kids;
- ⊕ financial stability;
- ⊕ respect.

You should now have a list of several things that make you happy. Do you see anything that these things have in common?

I have found that in the majority of cases, all the things that a man seeks for his self-esteem fall into one of three categories — what I call the three P's: Prestige, Power, and Pleasure.

Prestige: The Need to Succeed

Men's self-esteem is more career-centered. A man's work — and this is just as true if his work is studying — is the focus of a man's life, the center core upon which his sense of self and ego is built. Success in the world of work is essential for his sense of well-being.[1]

For the male, "Who am I?" translates into "What have I accomplished?" A healthy ego — what I refer to as *Prestige* — is the measuring stick a man uses to determine his self-worth.

The need to achieve in order to be "someone" — to feel that they are significant in some way — is ingrained in people's nature. The need to succeed is a natural human drive. Most people feel compelled to achieve something — to acquire, build, succeed, produce, accomplish.

But Prestige is especially important to men. Do others see me as somebody, as a success, maybe even unique? Unlike women, whose drive to succeed is about feeling accomplished, for a man it's about feeling accomplished,[2] while for a man it's about how others perceive him. He craves the respect he gets for his success. He feels fulfilled when people think highly of him.

---

1. Dr. Miriam Adahan, *It's All a Gift* (Feldheim Publishers, 1992), p. 106.
2. See Chapter 3, "Women and the Three A's."

A wealthy man nearing the end of his life called his lawyer. "After my demise," he told him, "give twenty-five thousand dollars to every employee in my company."

"Sir," said the lawyer, "your company is only five years old. It has hardly any employees."

"True, but can you imagine how good it will look in the newspapers?"

Since Prestige is all about how others perceive you, men set their self-worth according to who they know and how important their friends and acquaintances are: With whom do I rub shoulders? Am I connected to important politicians, well-known rabbis, celebrities, or statesmen? Am I accepted by my wealthier neighbors and peers? Which university did I attend? Which rabbinical academy did I graduate from? Did I make it to the dean's list or into *Who's Who*?

This drive to appear successful can manifest itself in different ways at different stages of life. With children, it may motivate a child to be popular, to excel in sports, or to get top grades. It can also manifest itself in negative ways. A boy may steal to buy candy for his friends to gain popularity, or he might cheat on a test to hide his learning disability.

When he grows up, a man's need to succeed is reflected in the car he drives, the smartphone he owns, the career he has, the size of his house, and the number and length of his vacations. Taken to the extreme, this can bring a man to resort to desperate measures to maintain his image: accruing serious debt, lying, cheating, and stealing.

An immigrant couple from Russia won the lottery soon after they arrived in America. Suddenly their life changed drastically. In Russia, they had been simple farmers and had very little knowledge of world culture. Now they lived in a fancy neighborhood where all the movers and shakers lived. They moved in the upper-class circles, getting invited to formal dinner parties and hobnobbing with powerful people.

When they became part of this elite group, they realized how ignorant they were. They began to read books and educate themselves and learn as much as they could so they could keep up with their new friends.

The next time they went out to dinner, the topic turned to Beethoven. Enthusiastically, people stated their opinions about his music. In the middle of the conversation, the Russian woman called out, "Beethoven, yes! A wonderful composer and nice person. Just yesterday, I met him on the number 3 train going from Manhattan to Queens." Her husband gave her a kick under the table, letting her know that she'd blown it.

A couple of minutes later, his wife left the table to visit the powder room. Her husband also excused himself, blushing with embarrassment. He walked quickly toward the powder room, and before his wife could enter, he whispered, "Natasha! What's wrong with you? You couldn't have met Beethoven on the number 3 train. It doesn't go to Queens!"

For the religious Jew, the drive for Prestige may manifest itself differently. Am I considered knowledgeable in Torah? Would people say I am a Torah scholar? What novel insights have I developed? How deep is my relationship to my rabbi? Do I feel connected to G-d? Am I achieving the purpose for which I was created? Do I feel inspired by this way of life?

In addition, regardless of whether a man is nonobservant or religious, his ego is also influenced by the person he marries (her status and appearance), his kids (whether they are cute or smart or pretty), and his position in the community. The fact is, how his peers perceive him, his personality, and his achievements exert a powerful influence on his feelings of self-worth.

Jackie Mason often spoke about the father of a Jewish truck driver. When asked, "What does your son do for a living?" he replied proudly, "My son is a lifesaver."

"What type of lifesaving does he do?" the friend asked.

"Could you imagine if a truck rolled onto the highway without a driver, how many innocent people could be hurt? Well, my son is the guy who jumps into the driver's seat and grabs the steering wheel to prevent it from happening. He's responsible for saving hundreds of lives every day!"

Power: Do Others Recognize My Strength?

From the time they are little boys, men relate to each other asymmetrically, either one-up or one-down. In any encounter, men quickly establish who is more dominant, powerful, and successful. In a marriage, the man wants the person to be him.[3]

The second P stands for Power. It, too, is integral to a man's self-esteem. Power is manifested by the feeling of control over situations, people, and outcomes.

Do I project a forceful image? Do my peers respect me? How much power does my job give me? Does my wife feel that I am the Man of the House? Do I provide her with security and project strength? Would she call on me to trap a mouse? (Well, maybe that is an exception. We might have to call the exterminator.) Do my children see me as a hero? Are they trying to emulate me? In school, do they mention me with pride?

When a man is young, this need for power may manifest itself as bullying. Pushing around his peers and poking fun at weaker kids gives him a sense of strength and control.

---

3. Adahan, *It's All a Gift*, p. 102.

Later, when he reaches his teenage years, the pursuit of Power evolves into a need to be perceived as macho. This term is applied to men for good reason. Muscles and physical strength make a man feel powerful. How much weight he can lift while bench-pressing is a measure of his self-worth. Can I carry those heavy suitcases? How slick am I at maneuvering the car around the curves? How much alcohol can I imbibe without getting drunk? This is also why famous boxers, baseball players, football players, and hockey stars earn men's respect for their prowess and strength, and why men try to emulate them.

> When men grow up, they primarily seek Power in two areas: at home and in their careers. Some men need to feel that their opinion is the final one in the house. The kids wouldn't dare question their father or think of disobeying him. Nothing is negotiable. The man needs to feel he is in total control.[4]
>
> Men are willing to share power, but they still want to see themselves as the most powerful, and as having the final decision. Most women will oblige, if they feel their husbands love them. A man who is interested in power but not love will destroy his marriage.[5]

In the office, the man wants to feel that people listen to him, that his opinion counts. For some men, this is so important that they may not be able to take orders from superiors because "I won't be pushed around." They need to be the boss.

---

4. Honoring parents is an important principle in Judaism; children are expected to respect their parents and obey them without question. At the same time, Judaism doesn't condone parents acting as tyrants and warns parents not to act in a way that will provoke their children to disrespect them.

5. Adahan, *It's All a Gift*, p. 106.

The fact is that criticism often derives from the husband's own needs to feel strong and obeyed.[6]

There is another integral aspect to the drive for power, and that is buying power. You might think that having money itself is a male need. The truth is that money has no intrinsic value to a man. Its value is linked to what it can buy. He thinks, *The larger my bank account, the stronger I feel. My money can buy me anything, and people respect me more when they know how wealthy I am.* A mansion is a sign of economic strength. A luxury car gives men a feeling of importance. The yacht, the Rolex, the designer clothes are all different ways for a man to show his power and gain prestige.

For men, their self-worth is so tied to finances that when there is a financial crisis, most men feel depressed and may even hit rock bottom. When men associate their worth with money, business, assets, bank accounts, and investments, they risk having their self-esteem crushed every time the stock market drops.

Here is a parable to put this idea into perspective:

Once there was a dog that was cherished by his old master. When the dog realized that his master was about to die, he knew that his comfortable life was over and he'd have to fend for himself. He asked his master how he could protect himself from the ferocious beasts in the woods.

The owner made a costume for the dog. The top half looked like a lion, and the bottom half resembled a bear. When the dog went into the forest, the animals were very curious about this strange new creature. They quickly informed the lion, king of the animals, about it. He summoned the dog to his cave.

"Who are you?" questioned the lion.

"My grandfather was a lion," the dog said confidently.

---

6. Rabbi Aharon Feldman, *The River, the Kettle, and the Bird* (Feldheim Publishers, 1987), p. 51.

"But who are you?" the lion asked a little louder.

"My grandmother was a bear," said the dog, a little less confidently.

"WHO ARE YOU?" roared the lion.

Meekly, the hound said, "I am just a dog."

Men want people to see the lion or bear that they show to the world. They seek to emphasize their strengths and shy away from displaying their weaknesses and vulnerabilities. Taken to the extreme, the drive for power produces dictators, abusive CEOs, and inflexible and controlling husbands.

Pleasure: It Makes Me Feel Good

THE THIRD *P* IN the equation is *Pleasure*. The pursuit of pleasure, and the desire to feel good, is generally considered to be a masculine trait. The saying goes that the best way to a man's heart is through his stomach. Men have well-known appetites for physical pleasures: good wines, juicy steaks, rare whiskey, and cold beer.[7]

Males' well-known interest in marital relations is motivated by physical pleasure. I believe most people would agree that men provide love in exchange for physical intimacy, while women provide physical intimacy in exchange for love.[8]

Obviously, all humans seek pleasure. We all — men and women alike — enjoy eating, sleeping, and having a good time. But men's pursuit of pleasure is fundamental.

---

7. According to the Bureau of Labor Statistics 2010–11 annual report, single men spent an average of $507 on alcohol per year, while single women spent less than half that amount, $216.

8. See also the next chapter, "Women and the Three A's."

A man in his eighties had a thorough medical examination. When he was done, he asked the doctor, "Do you think I'll live to be a hundred?"

"Do you smoke?" the doctor asked.

"No," he replied.

"Do you drink or eat fatty foods?" the doctor asked.

"No."

"Do you gamble?"

"No."

"So why do you want to live so long?"

I should mention that the three P's often overlap. One's job can be a source of prestige and power. Men are notorious for following competitive sports; this gives them both Power and Pleasure. Buying a new car represents Prestige, especially if it's expensive. It also represents Power because the driver is in control, and driving a new car is a pleasurable experience. In fact, we find that it is primarily men who enjoy car racing, horse racing, extreme sports, piloting fighter planes, and joining special units in the army. These activities fulfill a man's need for Power, Prestige, and Pleasure.

> When a man opens the car door for his wife, you can be sure that either the car is new or the wife is new.

When I shared my ideas on Prestige, Power, and Pleasure with a community member, she said, "You are basically depicting men as vain egocentrics who are mainly concerned about themselves. But I know some very caring and giving husbands."

"What you say is correct," I answered. "But these men have their innate natural drives. They have refocused their lives on their spouses and family, and these men will generally have good marriages and a strong bond with their loved ones. The point I am making is that men typically pursue the three P's unless they have been educated otherwise or trained themselves to focus on people and relationships outside of those pursuits."

Also, a man usually changes as he ages. This is not to say that the three P's vanish entirely, but they begin to be less important as males get older, and their family, community, and religious beliefs take on greater importance.

The reality at every stage of life is this: Males need a healthy self-esteem, and when one of the things that provides it is missing, most males try to replace it with something else.

Men seek Prestige, Power, and Pleasure for their self-esteem.

---

3 Women and the Three A's

WOMEN ALSO NEED HEALTHY self-esteem for their well-being. But the things that give the women a sense of self-worth are very different than for men. If you are a woman reading this, make a list of the things that make you feel good about yourself. Here are some possible items:

⊕ a good marriage;
⊕ a nice family;
⊕ a few less pounds;
⊕ an outfit that makes me look good;
⊕ new shoes;
⊕ my friends.

If you examine your list, you'll find that a woman's self-esteem is typically connected to what I call the three A's: Achievement, Appearance, and Affection.

I Achieve, Therefore I Exist

Even when American women work outside the home, they still report that their major source of fulfillment is their family.[1]

Every woman needs to feel that she is achieving something in this world. Regardless of whether she puts her effort into her home or career, she needs to feel that she is not wasting her time.

---

1. Adahan, *It's All a Gift*, p. 106.

Not feeling a sense of achievement is tantamount to not existing.

In a society where people are taught about the importance of self-realization, it goes without saying that women are also going to seek prestige and power. However, overall, women are less power-hungry than men, and although they want to feel successful in their careers and achievements, it usually isn't about an ego trip. Just consider how many women with college degrees choose to stay home and take care of their children instead of pursuing a career and letting someone else care for the children.

In today's society, many women understand "achievement" to mean that they must pursue a career in the business world. But there are many women who take a great deal of pride in raising families. Years ago I came across this story:

> "It's been over twenty years," said the man to his friend, "and every time I see you in the mall, you're holding your wife's hand. "Well," the friend replied, "if I let go, she shops."

A woman went to a government office to fill out a form. For "Profession," she wrote "Mother." When she handed in the form, the clerk saw what the woman had written and made a face. The next time she had to fill in her profession, the woman wrote, "Judge, doctor, psychologist, and administrator." She was pleased to see how the clerk received her this time.

When she finished telling her story, she said, "I wasn't exaggerating." When one of her children accused the other of starting a fight, she had to play the role of judge and decide who was the guilty party. When her kids fell sick, she became their doctor. And she often had to serve as a psychologist and administrator in order to help with her family's various needs.

A woman's need to feel that she is achieving and making a difference in some way or another is not the same as an ego trip. Men feel a need to achieve for the prestige. Women do so in order to feel fulfilled.

Appearances Do Matter to Me

BEGINNING EARLY IN CHILDHOOD, females are more concerned about their appearance than males.[2]

The second A, Appearance, is often associated with women. Though men also like to look good and appreciate beautiful objects, appearance and beauty are more important to women. Want proof? Check out how much space the men get in the walk-in closet. Count the pairs of shoes women own compared to men. Typically, men are not quite as interested in their appearance as women, and this is reflected in the way they dress and live.

> The doorbell rings and Ben Levy opens the door. He is a little surprised to see a deliveryman with seven hatboxes. "This is for Mrs. Levy," the man says.
>
> "Sara," Mr. Levy calls out, "did you order seven hats?"
>
> "Yes, of course," comes her reply.
>
> "Why in the world do you need seven hats?" he asks his wife.
>
> "To match my seven new outfits, of course!"

Look at the cosmetics industry. There are countless more products — creams, makeup, shampoos, perfumes — made for women than for men. According to data provided by beauty clinics, 78 percent of their clients are women. Women are much more willing to change their looks via surgery than men — 90 percent of cosmetic surgeries are performed on women, as opposed to a mere 10 percent of men.[3]

Young women also typically desire to lose weight, while

---

2. Feldman, *The River, the Kettle, and the Bird*, p. 47.

3. The American Society for Aesthetic Plastic Surgeries, www.surgery.org/media/statistics.

young men, in order to look masculine, are more likely to want to gain weight — those who do want to lose extra pounds tend to try to achieve this through exercise rather than dieting. Women, by contrast, will starve themselves and try all sorts of exotic, and even unhealthy, methods to lose weight and achieve a slim physique. Of all the people who suffer from anorexia and bulimia, only 10 percent are men.[4]

Furthermore, the majority of men who undergo weight-loss surgery are generally more concerned about their health than their looks. I realize that this is a great generalization, but it appears to reflect a basic truth: Most women are more concerned about their appearance than men.

> Of course, female concern with appearance only intensifies as the girl matures, and one of her highest priorities throughout life is her appearance.[5]

Shopping, a favorite pastime for many women, is also connected to their need to look good. Women dress for their self-esteem, and they appreciate when people acknowledge how well they dress.[6]

We can find support for this point in a biblical verse. The Torah states, "A man should not wear the clothes of a woman, and

4. The National Eating Disorders Collaboration, *An Integrated Response to Complexity: National Eating Disorders Framework* 2012; S. Paxton, "Do Men Get Eating Disorders?" *Everybody Newsletter* (1998), p. 41; G.C. Patton et al., "Adolescent Dieting: Healthy Weight Control or Borderline Eating Disorder?" *Journal of Child Psychology and Psychiatry and Allied Disciplines* 38 (1997): 299–306.

5. Feldman, *The River, the Kettle, and the Bird*, p. 47.

6. According to a survey by eBates and TNS Global, "More than half of Americans, both men and women, are guilty of using retail therapy to lighten their moods… Almost 64 percent of women admit to shopping to lighten their mood, spending money, in ranking order, on clothes, food, and shoes. Men in the survey shopped most for food, electronics, and music or movies when they wanted a pick-me-up.

a woman should not wear the clothes of a man."[7] The Talmud explains[8] this to include that a man should not be overly concerned about his physical appearance, while the prohibition that a woman should not wear male clothes applies to armor and weapons. It seems that the Torah, too, relates women to appearance and men to strength and power.

> While men are also interested in their clothing, that perspective is decidedly different. Through their clothing, women tend to communicate the message, "Please look at me." Men's clothing, in contrast, is meant to gain respect and prestige or to display a certain image: young, rich, et al.[9]

A man came in late to the office for the third time in a week. "If you don't give me a good excuse, you're fired," said his boss.

"I have a great excuse. The alarm clock didn't go off. When I opened my eyes, it was already eight a.m. I woke up my wife and asked her if she could give me a ride to work. We got ready in ten minutes and rushed out.

"The Brooklyn Bridge was closed, so I jumped into the Hudson and swam across the river. I got out, bought a new suit, jumped onto a passing police motorcycle and got here as soon as I could."

"You're lying," the boss said.

"Why do you say that?"

"No woman can get ready in ten minutes."

---

7. Deuteronomy 22:5.

8. Talmud, *Nazir* 59a; see *Shulchan Aruch, Yoreh Deah* 182:5.

9. Feldman, *The River, the Kettle, and the Bird*, p. 48.

The Love That I Crave

A woman's most deep-seated need, the one which shapes her personality and attitude toward life more than anything else, is her need to be loved, admired, and respected.[10]

The third and strongest of the A's is *Affection*. Even prior to marriage, girls seek to establish an emotional connection with their contemporaries more than boys do. Girls are more involved with making friends and social connections than boys are. For boys, a friend is someone to do something with rather than someone they need to connect with. Their friendships are based on a mutual preference for sports, games, or playing pranks. Girls look to connect and develop serious relationships.

Over the years, I have asked dozens of women in my congregation, many of whom come to me with their *chatanim* (fiancés) for pre-wedding counseling, what it is that they look for in marriage. Virtually all of them answered that they want to be loved. A woman's need to feel loved is a major part of her sense of self-worth. Feeling cherished and loved is as important to a woman's emotional well-being as oxygen is vital to the body.

We find this idea in the Torah. When Yaakov's wife, Leah, bore his first son, she named him Reuven, "for now G-d saw my affliction and now I will be loved."[11] Similarly, the Talmud states that in general, "A woman prefers to be married to a man who is not her ideal husband rather than stay single."[12] This is because a woman has such a vital need for company. More than being rich or famous, her self-esteem is dependent on having a husband who cares about her.

---

10. Ibid., p. 46.
11. Genesis 29:32.
12. Talmud, *Yevamos* 118b.

Similarly, the Mishnah states that a woman prefers one *kav*, a small measure, of sustenance and a good relationship rather than nine *kavim* of sustenance but an unfulfilling relationship.[13] When a woman feels someone cares for her and takes care of her, she feels emotionally strong and healthy. When she feels ignored and taken for granted, she becomes stressed and anxious.

This explains why women like to talk to other women about their problems. It's not about gossiping, it's about connecting. For the same reason, if they feel that their husbands don't understand them, they will gravitate toward someone who does.

This reminds me of a true story that happened to a couple of members of my congregation. Pesach was arriving and the house was in disarray. While the wife worked feverishly to make everything ready, her husband went to work as usual. On the day before Pesach, she couldn't take it anymore. "Don't you see me slaving away?" she scolded. "Can't *you* do something?"

Caught by surprise, the husband said, "What's your problem? You know I've been working hard in the office and that you're in charge of the Pesach preparations."

"I realize you're busy," she said. "But surely you can do something in your own home for Pesach!"

"Tell me what you need and I'll be glad to do it," the husband said.

"You have eyes. Look around and figure out what needs to be done. Why do I need to explain the obvious?"

"My brain works differently; I need to be told exactly what you need."

The following year, the husband remembered his wife's frustrations. A few weeks before Pesach, he said to her, "What can I do for Pesach?"

---

13. Mishnah, *Sotah* 3:4.

"Nothing. Thanks for the offer, but I can handle it."

He couldn't believe it. Last year, he had been rebuked for not offering his help. A year later, his wife declined his offer without batting an eyelash. What had changed?

What his wife had really been seeking was not help with the cleaning, but support. She wanted to know that her husband realized how hard she was working. It wasn't necessary for him to do anything but acknowledge her. She just wanted proof that he wasn't taking her for granted.

Now that we know about the three A's, it's interesting to note that according to the Torah, a man must provide his wife with three things: food, clothing, and marital relations.[14] In my opinion, these correspond to two of the A's: Appearance and Affection.

The connection between clothes and Appearance is obvious. Similarly, the connection between intimacy and Affection is self-understood. In fact, the word that the Torah uses for "intimacy" is *onah*.[15] Literally translated, the word means "time" and refers to a woman's cycles. Perhaps by using this word, the Torah is telling us that the priority is for men to regularly spend time with their wives and endeavor to fulfill their need for love and affection.

Before I go on to discuss how the P's and A's affect relationships, I want to acknowledge that in today's society, it's possible to find a woman who will pursue Prestige and Power and a man who will have a need for Affection or a nice Appearance. Even so, the basic premise of this book applies: Women in general are more emotionally in tune than men and seek more emotional

---

14. See Exodus 21:10.
15. Exodus 21:10 and Ibn Ezra there.

closeness in relationships than their husbands, and being aware of this difference is an important element for a fulfilling marriage.

Women want to feel accomplished, are interested in their appearance, and seek affection as a means of enhancing their self-esteem.

4 When the P's Meet the A's

E ARLIER, WE ESTABLISHED THAT happiness is at the top of the pyramid of our pursuits. For us to achieve this goal, we need to have a healthy and solid self-esteem. We also stated that both men and women consciously and subconsciously seek to constantly reinforce their self-worth constantly in different ways: he with the three P's and she with the three A's.

What fuels a man's self-esteem differs greatly from what a woman needs to boost her self-image. This is why, when G-d gave the Torah to the Jewish nation, He commanded Moshe to speak to the men and women differently. Moshe was told to speak to the women softly and to speak to the men sternly.[1] Since men understand power, Moshe was told to talk to them with resolve. Show them who is boss. Women are more interested in connecting. Talk politely and you can achieve more than you can with words of force.

So what does this mean for marriage? Does this really make any difference?

Absolutely. Since a man pursues Prestige, Pleasure, and

---

1. See Rashi's commentary on Exodus 19:3.

Power, he assumes that his wife needs the same things to give her a sense of self-worth. The woman assumes that the man needs affection and fulfillment (Achievement) in the same way she needs it. Each is unaware of the different needs of the other. And that's where the trouble starts.

> One night, a woman found her husband standing over their baby's crib. Silently she watched him as he looked down at the sleeping infant. She saw a mixture of emotions cross his face: delight, amazement, enchantment. Touched by this unusual display of emotion, she said, "A penny for your thoughts." "It's amazing," he said. "I just can't believe anybody could make a crib like that for only forty-six dollars!"

People have a hard time satisfying needs they are unaware exist. Can you imagine describing the color blue to someone who is blind? How about explaining the satisfaction of being a father to a teenager? Can anyone truly appreciate anything without experiencing it?

So while the man is pursuing everything that will boost his self-esteem — his three P's — he is probably simultaneously (though unintentionally) neglecting to provide the elements his wife needs for her self-esteem, *because he doesn't realize that her needs are so different from his.* His wife is unable to fathom why her husband is so uncaring of her needs; she becomes offended and upset, which leads to nagging and dissatisfaction.

So What's Better?

ONE OF MY FAVORITE exercises that I assign to the graduating class that I teach in the Albert Einstein School in Panama goes like this (you can do this exercise, too):

Rabbi Laine: "Which school is better? The Albert Einstein School or the other Jewish schools in town?"

Students: "The Albert Einstein School is superior."

RL: "What would you prefer to be, a Panamanian or Colombian?"

Students: "Panamanian." (The ones from Venezuela say, "Venezuelan.")

RL: "Is it better to be a man or a woman?"

The boys say: "A man." The girls reply: "A woman."

RL: "Is it preferable to be an Ashkenazi or a Sephardi?"

The Ashkenazim say: "Ashkenazi." The Sephardim reply: "Sephardi."

Then comes the most important question: "Are the answers you gave based on your intellect or emotions and instinct?"

At least some students argue that their answers were based on their intellect. By the end of the class, however, they usually agree that their answers were almost always based on emotion and instinct.

We tend to defend what we consider ours. Furthermore, what we consider "ours" somehow defines our self-esteem. My school, my country, my team, my gender, my culture, by extension means "my ego." This plays itself out in so many marriages. It may concern *my* mom's cooking, *my* family culture, *my* school, *my* way of doing things, *my* vision. The point is that it is this underlying attitude that creates difficulties in the relationship. Not only is the man pursuing his three P's, even if he knows that his wife has different needs, he may not understand why these needs are so important to her.

The woman may not understand why it's so essential for her husband to drive himself for Power, Prestige, and Pleasure over other things that she considers important. They each think their needs, their perceptions, are the right ones and their spouse should want the same things because "my pursuits are surely more rational and basic."

Of course, this is not the case, and conflicts arise as a result.

Let's go back to the classroom. What is the correct answer to the questions I asked the students? There are good things about my school and good things about the other school. There are benefits to being Panamanian and advantages to being Colombian. Each gender, culture, and team has virtues and defects. No one is perfect, but you can find the good in everything.

The Sages in the Mishnah tractate of *Avot* put it this way: "Who is wise? He who learns from everyone."[2] Many people are self-obsessed and have a hard time seeing any value in anyone else. To be able to see noble qualities in every person truly is a sign of wisdom.

In my experience, this is the crux of many marital problems, regardless of whether the couple has been together for two years or eighteen years. They are invariably linked to this formula: Men need the three P's to make them happy, women need the three A's, and neither of them understands the other's needs and is therefore unable to fulfill them.

How Men View Women	How Women View Men
A businessman is dynamic; a businesswoman is aggressive.	She's an achiever; he's power-hungry.
He's good with details; she's fussy.	She's confident; he's obstinate.
When he's depressed it's justified; when she's moody it must be her cycle.	She shares her views; he's opinionated.
He thinks quickly; she's reckless.	She has full control; he's bossy.

---

2. *Avot* 4:1.

More than Communication — Empathy

MEN EXPRESS ANGER EASILY because anger signifies a willingness to fight and a way of declaring, "I'm in control. I'm superior."

> To him, she's overreacting; to her, he's insensitive.
>
> To him, her "excessive" emotional response indicates that she is unstable and immature, so he criticizes her for being overly emotional, which shatters her further.
>
> To a woman, a man's commanding voice, endless instructions, and constant criticism are indications that he is insensitive, boorish, uncaring, and cruel.[3]

Often marital issues are focused on communication. If only they could communicate better, their marriage would improve. If they just told each other how they really feel, everything would be solved. But it's not just about communication. Before communication comes empathy.

It was the middle of a very cold winter in Russia. Zalman, one of the wealthiest members of the community, was snug at home, sitting before the huge fireplace that generated plenty of heat for his entire house. As he sat, enjoying the cozy warmth, someone came knocking on the door. The butler was surprised to see the rabbi of the city standing outside at such a late hour and in such bad weather.

Butler: "Please come in, Rabbi."

Rabbi: "Would you mind calling Zalman to the door?"

Butler: "Rabbi, it's quite cold. Wouldn't you like to get warm?"

Rabbi: "Thanks, but I am in a rush. Please call Zalman. I will be brief."

Zalman came to the door in his slippers and shirtsleeves.

Zalman: "Rabbi, would you like to come in?"

---

3. Adahan, *It's All a Gift*, p. 101.

Rabbi: "No, thanks, I will just be a minute. As you can see, Zalman, the winter is bitter. Our city has many poor people who can't afford wood to make fires in their homes."

Zalman: "Excuse me, Rabbi, it's cold. Do you mind if we talk over a hot cup of coffee?"

Rabbi: "I'm in a rush, so please give me thirty more seconds. The price of wood has skyrocketed this year, and the poor people are having an extremely difficult time purchasing the wood. Now you know what happens to a home that has no firewood. It's freezing all the time."

By this point Zalman had started to shake from the cold. "Rabbi, please come inside. I can't stand the cold. It's penetrated my bones!"

"If you insist, I will come in," the rabbi said. He stepped inside and immediately continued his speech. "We need to collect ten thousand rubles to keep the poor people of the city warm."

"Of course I will help," Zalman exclaimed. He quickly went to his desk and wrote a check for the entire amount.

The rabbi thanked him for his generosity and turned to leave.

"Rabbi, before you leave, I have one question," Zalman asked. "If you came to me for money, you surely realized that this would take more than one minute. Why didn't you come in right away?"

"My dear Zalman," the rabbi replied, "I wanted you to actually feel the cold. If you don't feel the pain of others, you won't be as generous!"

This story illustrates an important point emphatically, but for one thing: We can all relate to how it feels when we're cold, *but it's much more difficult to identify with something outside our emotional makeup.* This is unmistakably what creates so much anxiety and stress in many relationships.

Most men have a hard time relating to this truth, and understandably so, because it makes so little sense in the man's brain. They don't even realize that women need different things than they do.

Many women complain, "I don't have the emotional closeness I want with my husband." … In fact, there is a physiological basis for this complaint. Numerous research studies have confirmed that the brains of men and women are organized quite differently. One major difference is that the emotional center in a man's brain is located specifically in the right hemisphere. In contrast, the woman's emotional capacities reside in both.[4]

Women have an easier time plugging into what their spouses need, but they can't understand why their husbands won't do the same for them. They can't fathom why their spouses are so oblivious, and at times insensitive, to their emotions and needs. Women have a need to feel loved and cared for; they need the other person to want to spend time with them and let them know they're loved. They can't figure out why men don't understand this need and are so reluctant to supply it.

In most cases, they both love each other, but because they have different expectations, they are working on the relationship at cross purposes. This creates much confusion and dissatisfaction in a marriage.

Two old friends met after many years. They began chatting about their lives and families. "How is your daughter?" Hannah asked Janet.

"My daughter is married and doing very well. She is very lucky. Her husband takes very good care of her. He lets her sleep in and brings her breakfast in bed. For lunch they go out to the finest restaurants. He gives her plenty of shopping money. For dinner they also go out to dine on the best cuisine.

"And how about your son?" she asked.

"My son also got married, but he wasn't so fortunate. His

---

4. Adahan, *It's All a Gift*, p. 107.

wife is lazy. She refuses to get up in the morning and expects
to get breakfast in bed, and for lunch and dinner she eats only
in restaurants! Can you believe it?"

Before the wedding of one of my congregants, I visited his
parents at their home. When I mentioned to the groom that he
needed to educate himself about married life, he replied, "I can
speak to my father. My parents have an excellent marriage." The
expression on his mother's face clearly indicated that things were
not always as they appeared.

The boy's parents had been married for thirty-five years. Still,
the mother's knee-jerk reaction was, "You don't know what takes
place behind the scenes."

I interjected, "You should ask your mother for advice."

I knew that his mother would be able to guide him to understanding the needs of a woman more than his father, who had
learned about marriage the same way all men do — by trial and
error. Inevitably there would be flaws in his methods that could
be avoided by speaking to a woman.

You Have to Walk a Mile in Their Shoes

A WOMAN ONCE CAME to my office to share her marital woes with
me. The fundamental issue was that she didn't feel loved. When
she conveyed this message to her husband, he said, "How can you
say that? Look how much money you get to spend each month!"

He was confident that he was a good husband. In his mind,
he had proven that he loved his wife beyond the shadow of a
doubt by taking care of her credit card bills.

I explained to her my theory of the three P's and the three
A's. "I fully understand your point," I said. "Your husband is not
able to see your perspective. One of the three P's is Power, which
is strongly connected to money. In your husband's mind, sharing

his money in unlimited amounts with you is the greatest expression of his love."

To change her husband was going to take a lifetime, and I did not succeed in getting him to give her the emotional support that she craved. But at least she was able to understand the root of the situation — that it was based on perception, not intention. Is it true that her husband didn't care about her? Of course not. But she wasn't getting the affection and attention she needed. Why not? Because he had no clue that she actually had this need. How could he understand the needs of a woman if he had never experienced those needs?

Difficulty in understanding another's needs isn't restricted only to men. A woman once told me that she didn't believe that men seek the three P's.

"How do you know?" I said to her. "Only a man can tell you if the three P's theory is accurate."

Incidentally, her husband was at the same lecture. He heard her comment and my rebuttal, but remained quiet. (After all, who was he supposed to contradict, the rabbi or his spouse?)

A man went to his rabbi to arrange a divorce. "Baruch," said the rabbi, "you and your wife seem like such a great couple. Why are you thinking of getting divorced?"

"Rabbi," Baruch replied, "it's like my new pair of shoes. They look great on the outside, but only I know how they hurt on the inside!"

The Challenge

THE GREATEST CHALLENGE TO attaining this level of understanding is dealing with something that is so obvious to one person and yet so unfathomable to the other. Do I need to tell you to turn off the lights in the car? To turn off the air conditioning when you leave the room? To pay the phone bill before they cut off the line? That is how each spouse feels when the other questions their way of doing things, "Why do I have to explain myself? Isn't it obvious?" (Now that we are aware of this, however, we can be more understanding and maybe even try to give each other what we need.)

In some marriages, the tables are turned and the wife is the stronger personality. One might think that in such a scenario, the P's and A's theory does not apply. Although on the outside it appears that the roles are reversed, in my experience I have found that this is not so at all. Men and women maintain their nature and needs in most situations. It's just that they might also have the other's needs. A man might need more emotional support and a woman might seek power, but this does not diminish the fundamental emotional requirements that men and women generally have.

Men and women are different. What is obvious to one spouse is a mystery to the other. When a spouse misinterprets why the other reacts in a certain way, that's when troubles arise.

5 Self-Esteem Is Different for the Husband and Wife

S OMEONE I KNOW ONCE told his wife, "I love you, but I don't need you." What do you think about this statement?

To many men, the statement is very noble; it implies that the man has no ulterior motives. In other words, his relationship with her is unconditional. It's not based on anything he lacks.

Needless to say, the man's wife did not see it that way. To her this statement meant that she had no value. *If I am not needed,* she thought, *what is my worth?*

For most men, their spouse fulfills one (or more) of the P's on their list — Pleasure, Power, or Prestige. Obviously she fulfills his need for Pleasure, but she also can be a symbol of his Prestige or Power. To a man, most things in his life are fuel for his ego: the home he lives in, the car he drives, the watch he wears — and the wife he married. All of it contributes to his Prestige and Power. The woman he married is also a part of that.

> Whenever my husband says he has a good marriage, I always wonder who he married.

For women, a husband provides a large part of her self-esteem, especially the Affection that it's based on. Since she depends so much on her husband's affection for her self-worth, to hear that her husband "doesn't need her" can be very destructive. Since she needs her husband emotionally, she assumes that he feels the same way. By claiming that she is not needed, she feels that he is essentially saying, "If you disappeared tomorrow, it wouldn't be a big loss." This is not what he meant, but this is what she heard.

A Tale of Two Species

What Every Woman Expects	What Every Women Gets
A talented conversationalist	A conversation between commercials
A good listener with a good heart	Highly sensitive when she rebukes him; he has a great heart because he is always exercising, i.e., playing golf, bowling, etc.; and he listens, but only when she screams.
Someone who will help with household chores, shopping, and walking the dog	His way of helping in the house is reminding everyone to shut off the lights when leaving the room. He shops, but gets only half the list; and the last time he took out the dog, the dog disappeared.
Someone who has physical and mental strength	He has big muscles, but he is too busy for household needs.
Someone who is as smart as Einstein, but who is also handsome	He has heard of Einstein and he is considering a diet.

The Talmud teaches, "The woman's desire to marry is greater than a man's desire to marry."[5] Let's take a look at some statistics:[6]

---

5. Talmud, *Kesubos* 86.
6. Taken from The 2002 National Survey of Family Growth.

⊕ Over 70 percent of men and women aged 25–44 have been married: 71 percent of men and 79 percent of women.

⊕ The probability that men will marry by age 40 is 81 percent; for women, it is 86 percent.

⊕ A larger percentage of women than men aged 35–44 have married by age 35.

For many women, marriage is linked to their self-esteem, so for them getting married is a primary pursuit. For men, it's important to them to form a family, but they can achieve their self-esteem in other ways, so they don't feel the same need to marry.

Why Women Depend on Men for Their Self-Esteem

IN OUR DAY AND age, some people are convinced that there are no intrinsic differences between men and women. This discussion is not one that I will cover here in any great depth, since other authors address it and that is not the purpose of this book.[7] But I would like to touch upon how Judaism views male and female roles.

The book of Genesis discusses the first couple, Adam and Eve. The Torah tells us that G-d made every creature together with its mate. Adam, however, was born alone. Only later did G-d create Eve from Adam's body.

This is why most women desire to be connected to an appropriate male — what they like to refer to as their "soul mate." Since the female "stems" from the male, she feels complete when she is with him.

Adam, however, lived by himself until Eve was formed to

---

7. See, for example, Dr. Deborah Tannen, *You Just Don't Understand* (HarperCollins, 1990).

complement her husband. The female is an essential part of the male, but he can feel complete without a wife. From a slightly different angle, man is created from the earth. Therefore man feels connected to the earth — that is, to material pursuits. Women, by contrast, crave to reconnect to their origin — to a man.

Sociologically, men are independent by nature; their self-esteem does not depend on having a spouse. But a woman's self-esteem derives, to a large extent, from her husband. As a result, women may have a greater need for emotional intimacy than men and may want their husbands to spend more time with them. Men, as a rule, may be more assertive in seeking independence and individualism. This is their nature. It's not that they don't love their wives dearly, but at the same time, they need to have their own space.

How many wives think that their husband is more committed to the office than he is to his family? In the office he is alive and full of energy, but at home she doesn't see the same drive. And when the wife shares her observation with him, what is his immediate response?

"I am working and slaving away for the family. It's not that I don't want to spend more time with the family; I just can't. I need to work hard so I can support us, put the kids through college, travel, and secure a good retirement."

Now the wife feels guilty. *He is so right — he does work many hours and we do need the income.* But a part of her still feels that she is not his priority and she still wants to be the most important thing in his life.

Her instinct that she is not his only priority is partly on target. Yes, he is working to support the family, but he also works to fulfill his need for Prestige, Power, and Possessions. Chances are, even if he'd win the lottery or start making big bucks, he'd continue to work hard.

You may have seen this yourself: Many wealthy people, even with all the money they have, continue to work and create more businesses to generate more income, even though this costs them time they could otherwise spend with their families. This is because men have a drive to work to give them a sense of self-worth, and this usually comes before spending time with the family.

So what we have is a wild-goose chase. The wife seeks to feel good about herself, and therefore seeks her husband's time and attention. He, however, is nowhere to be found! He is looking for the things that will boost his own self-esteem, like more money, a successful career, and good connections.

Often, he reasons that he is doing all this for his wife, that she'll be happy if he brings home more money and becomes friends with higher-ups. And, in fact, he really believes that this is a good way to show his love, because he himself feels fulfilled from all these things, so why wouldn't she as well? She, too, will benefit. But if he'd ask her, he'd be surprised to know that if she had a choice, she would rather have his attention than his money.

It's Not Worth the Money

IN MORE THAN ONE instance, I have heard a woman say, "Feeling loved is worth more than all the luxury in the world and all the jewelry and clothes I could buy. If I had to choose a simple life with a person who truly loves me or a lavish lifestyle without love, I would take love over wealth any day."

This might not sound realistic, but this is the consensus of many women I have asked. The three A's mean more to women than the three P's. In addition, if they had to choose between one of the three A's over the other two, they'd prefer Affection.

I am not suggesting that material things are of no value to women. It's just not their primary need. If, however, her peers live a materialistic life, she won't want to feel left out or inferior to her neighbors. In this situation, the pursuit of material things will increase. In a way, this, too, is connected to her need for

Appearance. If she did not have those material things, she might feel inferior to her peers in her community and this would generate a great deal of anxiety.

Jack, a congregant and friend, told me a story that happened to him over fifty years ago, yet he still remembers the impact it had on his relationship as if it had just occurred.

"I went to the Far East to do business. My wife came with me. We went to dinner with one of my suppliers and had a couple of drinks. The way things were unfolding, I realized I could negotiate a better price for the goods I was buying. The hour was late and it was going to be a while before this deal would conclude, so I told my wife, 'Take a taxi to the hotel. I'll come later.'

"The negotiations went on until the wee hours of the morning, and I was able to bring down the price by half a million dollars. This was back in the sixties, so you can imagine how much I had profited.

"The next morning, when my wife woke up, I noticed she was upset. 'Berta!' I said, thinking to cheer her up. 'You won't believe it. We saved five hundred thousand dollars!'

"My words did not have the desired effect.

"'What's the matter, Berta?' I asked. 'Why so glum?'

"I was totally flabbergasted when I heard her answer. 'Why did you send me back to the hotel alone last night?'"

When I heard this story, I was blown away. Jack's wife had just heard that her husband had made a substantial amount of money, and all she had to do was return to the hotel alone. How could she be upset? Yet she was.

Do you think she overreacted?

The bottom line is that Berta felt abandoned. Yes, her husband had earned a huge sum of money, but that only served to demonstrate that she wasn't her husband's priority. Logically, she probably understood her husband's decision. Nevertheless, it did not change the emotional reality. In her mind, she felt slighted.

It's Not Enough That You Love Her

IT GOES WITHOUT SAYING that for any marriage to succeed, love is a vital ingredient. Usually, even if a couple is having trouble, they do love each other. But each claims that the other spouse doesn't love them at all. Is it possible that the same word means something so different for men than it does for women?[8]

Let's talk about men. How do they define "love"?

When a man feels respected and accepted for who he is, and has satisfactory marital relations, he feels that his marriage has a solid, loving foundation. He assumes that the same is true for his spouse. After all, if it seems to him that all is good, she probably feels the same way.

When the husband detects that his wife does not feel the same way as he does — when she expresses her dissatisfaction or acts resentful or disappointed — he asks himself, *What's wrong with her? She makes no sense. Don't I do enough for her? What does she want already?*

After racking his brain and not coming up with any justification, he concludes, "Something must be bothering her. She probably had a bad day. Maybe she had a fallout with a friend or it's that time of the month. But it can't have anything to do with me."

If he goes so far as to verbalize his belief, she responds, "You just don't understand. You'll never get it." In her mind she begins processing, *What is wrong with this man I married? I can't believe he really said this. He's trying to pretend that he isn't ignoring me and he hurt my feelings. He has some nerve shifting all the blame onto me!*

This leads to the thought, *It's clear that I'm not at the top of his list of priorities. I'm not a complicated person. All I expect from him is a little attention. Is it so much to ask from my husband? I just need to feel that he*

---

8. See Chapter 8, "Love Is Not an Accident," for the true meaning of love.

likes spending time with me, that my life is of interest to him, or, at the very least, that he notices that I am wearing a new pair of shoes!

Her husband, of course, does not expect this reaction. He is proud of himself. He finally detected that his wife was in a sour mood before she had to tell him. He made a thorough analysis, and it was clear that he didn't trigger this mood. So when she responds the way she does, he thinks, *This is not fair. Instead of congratulating me for showing my concern and care, all she can do is put me down. I can never win.* As a result he decides, *I will not make the same mistake again. In the future, I will just ignore her until she gets over her crisis.*

What is really happening here?

As long as the husband is in hot pursuit of his Prestige, Power, and Pleasure, and his understanding of a good relationship is so different from his wife's, she will never feel that she is his priority. For her, affection is one of her primary needs. When her husband does not spend time with her and show her affection in ways that *she* needs to be shown affection, she doesn't feel loved.

How is it possible for a husband to say, "Honey, you are my priority," and his wife doesn't believe it?

Do most men really think that their spouse is their priority? Of course. But this is true only on the rational and verbal levels. He believes and says that his wife is his priority, but his actions and the time he dedicates to his personal interests versus his marriage belie his words. In the reality of day-to-day life, he remains focused on Prestige, Power, and Pleasure.

In the husband's mind, he is a perfect spouse. He cares for his wife and is a responsible and hard worker. They own a home, pay their bills, and take a yearly vacation. He doesn't have any addictions and goes to the gym only twice a week. What could be wrong with such a husband? In the male brain, nothing. In the female brain, plenty. With all that, she'll say, "What about me? What about tending to my emotional needs? Yes, you are an excellent provider. But there's more to a marriage than stable finances. What about my emotional well-being?"

The man says, "You mean attention? I give you attention. Don't we spend time together when we are intimate?"

"Yes, but it's not enough!"

A woman needs to feel that she is *always* her husband's priority, and not just at a specific time or place. If she doesn't feel this, she will feel that she is lacking. Knowing that her husband makes her a priority is an integral part of her self-esteem. And for her to feel that she is his priority, she must get attention, affection, and appreciation from her spouse. When she doesn't, she feels down and may even become depressed.

I once mentioned this idea to a successful businessman whose business required him to do quite a bit of traveling. He said to me, "When I got married, I began to travel for the business and my wife became quite upset. I didn't understand why she was so anxious. I was the one who had to be away from home, and I was working quite hard. It came to the point that her mother offered to give me her business just so I would be able to stay in Panama and stop traveling. I refused the offer.

"Now I understand what was going on. While I traveled for my business and future, I was building my self-esteem. But my wife's self-esteem depended on my being there for her, which obviously was not happening.

"When we had our first child, everything changed. Now she became focused on the baby and their deep bond compensated for the affection she felt she was missing in her life because I was traveling. Recently our children moved out of the house and she has become very stressed again. Now I understand why."

Let's look at this from a different angle. Men work hard and often their jobs generate a lot of stress, so when they come home, they just want to relax. His idea of relaxing doesn't usually include his wife, and often if asked to share the details of what is causing him stress, he isn't willing to talk about it. So his wife wonders, *Why isn't he interested in spending time with me? Why doesn't he tell me what's bothering him? I'm his wife and I want to be there for him. Doesn't he understand that? What is wrong with our marriage?*

If she'd know about the three A's and the three P's, she would understand that he didn't choose to ignore her. He doesn't realize that she feels lacking. He believes that he is a wonderful husband because he refused a coworker's offer to grab a quick dinner at a local restaurant after working late. He thinks she should be thankful that he showed up for dinner and didn't burden her with extra worry. The result of this disconnect is confusion and conflict.

The Power of the Flower

If a man brings his wife flowers for no reason… there is always a reason.

Here is another story that illustrates the differences in sensibilities between men and women:

Michael and Debbie had a serious argument over who was responsible for paying the phone bill. The phone company had cut off their phone lines, and each one was sure it was the other's responsibility.

The environment at home was thick with tension. The next morning, Debbie realized that Mike was right. He had asked her to pay the bill and she had forgotten. What could she do to make it up to him? After all that was said the night before, it would not be easy to get the relationship back on track.

Suddenly, Debbie had an idea. Later that day, Mike received a letter of apology with an exquisite bouquet of flowers delivered to his office.

Do you believe this story? Would a woman try to fix a problem in her marriage with flowers? How about if the story were reversed? What if Mike was the one who had made the mistake and he sent the flowers to Debbie. Now does the story make sense?

When a man receives flowers, he either accepts them as something nice (but not very useful) or he thinks they are a waste of money (they're going to dry out in a couple of days anyway). When a woman receives roses, she feels terrific.

> A man goes to a florist and asks for a dozen roses.
>   Florist: "Is it for your wife's birthday?"
>   "No," the man replies.
>   Florist: "Maybe your anniversary?"
>   "No," he responds.
>   Florist: "Has she been sick?"
>   "No," the man says, shaking his head.
>   Florist: "Well, in that case I really hope she forgives you."

A friend of mine had just gotten married, and he was having a rough time in the beginning. I gave him some advice and it helped. One day, he called requesting to speak to me right away. We arranged to meet, and upon entering my home, he told me that he had argued with his wife and didn't know what to do about it. I listened carefully and then told him, "You are totally at fault."

"What should I do now?" he asked.

"Go to the florist, buy a beautiful bouquet of flowers, and write a nice card to your wife," I suggested.

"Rabbi," he responded, "you don't know my wife. This will not be enough. It won't work."

"Calm down and listen to me," I said. "Just do as I tell you."

A couple of months later I met him and asked, "How are things going?"

"Rabbi," he said, "your flower trick worked perfectly. She calmed down and things have been fine ever since!"

They went on to have a good marriage and a couple of more kids.

How can a flower be so powerful? One rose can defuse a

serious fight. To me it's almost illogical. If you ask a woman how this makes sense, she would most likely say, "That's how it is. It's a fact. Flowers make me feel good."

In light of the P's and the A's, it makes perfect sense. Flowers don't do anything for a man's Power, Prestige, or Pleasure. But they feed a woman's need for Affection. (It goes without saying that if your wife is allergic to flowers, don't insist on sending them to her. A woman once called me up, furious. "My husband just sent me two dozen long-stemmed roses," she complained. "What's wrong with that?" I asked. "I hate roses! I am allergic to them!")

It's Easier to Feel Neglected Than Loved

Nothing shocks a new wife more than the suspicion that her husband may not love her as much as she had hoped.[9]

When our self-esteem is low, we become moody, upset, anxious, and cranky. That is exactly what happens to a woman who does not feel that she is getting enough attention from her husband. When a woman feels down and ignored, she begins to re-evaluate her marriage.

She thinks, *My entire life I thought that when I got married, I would feel like a queen. The elation I experienced when we were engaged was so incredible that I was convinced that this would last forever. Now I realize that it was all an illusion.* Her conclusion: *How foolish I was to ever marry this person! Why did I fall for his sweet words? It's my fault.*

Her feelings for her husband have turned 180 degrees. She has

---

9. Feldman, *The River, the Kettle, and the Bird*, p. 48.

begun to blame him, telling herself, "He is a terrible person for doing this to me."

What do you think happens when they next sit down for dinner? She is so heated up that she is hard put to smile, much less fulfill his needs for prestige, power, or pleasure. In her view, she has been abandoned, so now she begins to reject him. He wants only to enjoy his dinner and the pleasant company of his wife. Her dissatisfaction is definitely not what he is looking for. So their marriage begins to deteriorate.

Incidentally, two outlets that women use when they are not feeling loved are... you guessed it, shopping and eating. Think about it. When a man makes his wife feel secure in his love, she doesn't need a substitute to boost her self-esteem. But a wife who feels neglected looks for something else to increase those good feelings. The easiest and most efficient way is either to eat or to shop — neither of which makes her husband happy, by the way.

There is a saying, "Identifying the disease is half the cure." It seems to me that the difference in the way that men and women pursue happiness and seek self-esteem is the core issue in marriage. There are many books out there that discuss the differences between the genders, explain common misconceptions and misunderstandings, and provide specific ideas and suggestions. But if they don't address the issue of self-esteem, I believe they're missing the essence of the problem.

Men don't necessarily need their wives for their self-esteem, as long as they have other ways to pursue Prestige, Power, and Pleasure. Since a woman needs affection for her sense of self-worth, her husband's attention and love are intrinsic aspects of her pursuit of happiness and self-esteem

6 She Wants to Talk, He Wants Space

W E LIVE IN A world that requires us to earn a living. Most people work forty hours a week, and many of them have another hour or two each day to commute. When they finally get home, they have dinner with the family and spend some time relaxing before retiring for the night.

I have asked dozens of men, "What do you like to do after dinner?" The most common answer is, "Watch television." In a home where there is no television, "Study or play with the kids" is the common response. Typically, men watch television, read the paper, or surf the Internet to relax. Other men go to the gym or go to some type of recreational sports club. In a religious home, men typically attend a class or learn Torah.

When I ask women the question "What do you like to do after dinner?" the consensus of most women is, "Talk." I mentioned this once in a class of men and women, and a woman turned to her husband and said, "You see, I'm not crazy!"

We Need to Spend Time Together

AFTER YEARS OF MARRIAGE, many women give up this dream of spending time with their spouse just talking about things. They get accustomed to the norm. They give up trying to have deep, mean-ingful conversations with them in order to feel closeness. Still, most wives would prefer to just talk over most other activities. But when they try, the following conversation usually takes place:

Wife: "Let's talk."

Husband: "Didn't we just talk?"

Wife: "When?"

Husband: "At dinner."

Wife: "What did we talk about?"

Husband: "You asked, 'How was your day?' I said, 'Pretty good,' and we chatted a bit."

Wife: "That's not talking, that's sharing information."

A woman thrives on sharing her life with her husband. She loves to tell him everything that happened to her during the time they were apart. The husband should listen with intent to what she has to say, even if it seems trivial and unimportant to him.[1]

For women, most conversations are exciting because the topic is secondary to the fact that they are spending time together. For men, sitting and chatting needs to be fulfilling and purposeful.

Most husbands try to be the best spouse in the entire world. Yet many are unsuccessful. What's more, they can't fathom what's wrong. They have tried everything they can think of to make their wives happy. When nothing seems to be working, they conclude that it must be their wives' fault!

After all, the man thinks, who can be a better husband than he? He makes a decent salary. He is a good provider and lets her spend generously. They dine out occasionally. They have domestic

---

1. Rabbi Shalom Arush, *The Garden of Peace*, p. 83 (reproduced with permission of the copyright holders, *Chut Shel Chessed* Institutions, 2008, Israel).

help in the home. His wife has plenty of time to relax. What more could any woman want?

Yet what does his wife say? "We need to spend more time together. We need to talk more. I feel we are drifting apart. Our relationship is not like it used to be. I am not your priority. You care about your clients more than about me."

Naturally the husband disagrees. "More time together? When? I work in the office all day. When I come home, we have dinner. Then I watch the news, catch up on sports, check out crucial Web sites for business, spend time helping the kids with their homework, and even tuck the little ones into bed. By the time I'm done, it's already eleven o'clock."

> "Sometimes I wish that I was one of the channels on our television," said a woman to her husband. "That way you would look at me once in a while."
> "Not a bad idea," he mused. "That way I could also change you occasionally."

Unsure of what his wife is trying to tell him, the husband tries to make her understand his perspective by repeating it.

"Look, you said that you wanted to talk. That's what we did during dinner. I asked about your day and you took ten minutes to tell me. You asked me how things went in the office and I told you in only three minutes. What else do we need to talk about?"

"Excuse me," she interjects, "you work for eight hours and all you can share with me is three minutes? I'm not being nosy. I just would love to hear about your day at the office."

"I don't like to bring work home. Anyway, it would be way too stressful for you."

"Don't worry about me," she says. "I really want to hear about your day."

"Trust me, you don't," he counters. "Let's leave it at that."

"But I enjoy talking with you. Not just about how your day went. Other issues as well."

"No problem," he responds, hoping to put the discussion to rest. "If there's anything I can do to help, I'm always available. You can count on me."

"I know that I can rely on you, but that's not what I mean. I just want to spend time with you!"

"Oh, now I understand," he says. "You want to spend time together. Okay. Why don't you join me when I watch the game? Or the news? Or anything — I mean, anything besides soap operas."

By this time, voices are beginning to rise. "Spending time with you doesn't mean watching television or sports. It means sitting and talking," she emphasizes.

Her husband replies in exasperation, "Do you see how you are going in circles? You want to talk. I explained to you that we do talk. You then claim that we don't spend time together. I come up with a great plan of how we can spend time together, and then what do you say? We need to talk more. Do you hear what you're saying?"

"You're the one who doesn't get it," she retorts. "Well, I'm done with trying to explain it to you."

Finally, he thinks, *this torture is over! She can't admit that she is wrong. This is her usual tactic: End the conversation by accusing me. What a relief she called it quits. She is lucky I married her — no one else would put up with this.*

His wife is thinking, *Why is my husband so thick-headed? I try to express my feelings, yet he always turns them around. What else could I have said? I was direct and to the point: "Let's spend some time talking." The only way he knows how to respond is to say how illogical I am. This is totally ridiculous. What luck, to marry a man who hasn't the faintest idea of how to have a relationship. If it weren't for me, our marriage wouldn't have lasted a week.*

Does this conversation sound familiar? I think that most of

us can identify with it on some level. The feelings expressed here are very common. If you and your spouse have never had this discussion, I'm impressed!

Malespeak 101

What He Says	What He Means
It's a male thing.	He has no explanation.
Oh, don't worry, it's nothing. It's just a little cut.	I am in pain and the blood is gushing out, but there is no way I am going to show any weakness.
I heard you.	I don't know what you said, but if I admit it, you will become angry, so I will try to convince you that I was paying attention.
We make a great team.	I like it when you keep the house organized, and when things are not the way they should be, I make sure to let you know.

She Craves Affection, He Craves Space

LET'S TAKE A DEEPER look at the conversation above. Given the information you have about the differences between men and women (the three P's vs. the three A's), can you identify the conversation that is actually taking place on a subconscious level?

The husband is saying, "My world revolves around Prestige, Power, and Pleasure, so after dinner, I will seek some activity that will fulfill one of these needs." What does he find to do? News, movies, sports, reading, or studying. The common denominator is entertainment, which equals "Pleasure" in the male world.

A woman's self-esteem depends on Achievement, Appearance, and Affection. However, feeling loved is the main ingredient.

When she marries, the self-esteem boosters of Achievement and Appearance don't compare to the need to feel loved. So after dinner, what does she want to do? Talk![2]

Doesn't she understand that they spoke at the dinner table? Of course, but what she really desires is affection, and this is achieved through connecting and talking. She needs to feel that her husband *wants* to spend time with her. *Talking* is the code word, and sitting together and communicating is the objective. She is even willing to talk about what went on in the office in order to spend time with her husband. But he is not interested. This, to him, is not conversation for the home. In his house, he would like to unwind. Eventually, when the option of watching a game together comes up, she rejects it. This is not my idea of attention, she feels.

> More often than not, nagging by a wife means that her husband is not paying her enough attention.[3]

Her husband doesn't realize that choosing another activity over spending time with his wife makes her feel bad. She automatically assumes that she is not his priority or even one of his interests. In her mind, she has not seen her husband for almost twelve hours! The fact that they can finally spend quality time together is exciting. So why doesn't he want to spend any time with her?

---

2. It is worthy to note that the Mishnah says explicitly that one should not converse excessively with one's wife (*Avot* 1:5). How does this fit with the idea that a man needs to spend time with his wife? We must take into consideration a simple fact. In the olden days, there weren't as many activities to do at home as there are today. So Judaism teaches that men need to remember that besides speaking to their wives, they should dedicate time to study Torah daily. In today's day and age, people aren't spending their time studying anyway. They are spending their time on many other things, so they should most definitely spend more time speaking to their wives.

3. Feldman, *The River, the Kettle, and the Bird*, p. 54.

I Love Her,
but I'm Watching TV Now

The same man who can give hours of his time to the community may complain that he cannot find five minutes for his wife or children. That's because when he gives to the community, he gets honor and prestige. Plus, he gives from his own initiative, which preserves his sense of control.[4]

When a man spends time with his wife, often it is at the expense of his pursuit of Prestige, Pleasure, and Power, so he finds it less desirable than other activities. He doesn't see what he would gain from just sitting and talking.

While I was in the middle of writing this book, I asked a group of men their opinions about the scenario I described above. Every man agreed that he had had similar conversations with his own wife.

One elderly individual told me that if his wife ever wanted to converse, he would tell her to go ahead and talk. If she needed to talk, he would listen. When the topic of television came up, I told this elderly gentleman how nice it was of him to listen to her — even on top of the noise coming from his favorite channel. He replied, "Yes, but she knows that when the news comes on, she can't interrupt." The class had a good laugh. He had affirmed my point: The news was more important than his wife's desire to converse.

Another man pointed out that he didn't mind listening to his wife when she talked about their children or grandchildren. I smiled. "In essence, you are agreeing with me," I told him. "When your wife shares information you want to hear, this falls into the category of Pleasure."

---

4. Adahan, *It's All a Gift*, p. 104.

> A man walks into a flower shop that has a sign on the door that reads, "SAY IT WITH FLOWERS." He asks the florist for a single rose.
> "Why do you want just one rose?"
> "I am a man of few words."

Another time, a newlywed called me on the phone. "How are things doing?" I asked.

"Okay, more or less," he said. Then he blurted, "My wife doesn't like it when I leave her at home twice a week while I go play tennis!"

I knew immediately what lay behind her dissatisfaction with her husband. He wanted pleasure: playing tennis with his friends. If it was about the exercise, he could have stayed home and run on the treadmill.

Meanwhile, his wife was begging him, "Stay home with me." She felt that tennis had become more important to him than spending time with her. It showed that she was not his priority. *I can accept that you are in the office most of the day*, she probably reasoned to herself. *But the evening is my time, so none of your hobbies should come at my expense.*

In short, for their self-esteem, men don't need to be with their wives for more than a limited amount of time. But a woman needs to feel loved and cared for constantly. As we said in the previous chapter, she complements his self-esteem, while he is part of her self-esteem.

> Husband: "Did you hear? They say that women speak twice as much as men."
> Wife: "Of course, because men don't listen."
> Husband: "WHAT did you say?"
> Wife: "See what I mean?"

We Both Love to Talk —
but about Different Things

THE TRUTH IS, MEN do like to talk. When the "boys" go out for a drink, do they talk or just drink? Of course they talk. If men love to talk so much, why don't husbands and wives talk more to each other?

Men and women typically have different areas of interest. If you'd ask men about their favorite topics of conversation, their list would probably include sports, business, cars, current events, and movies. If you'd ask women about *their* favorite topics of conversation, their list would probably look like this: fashion, beauty tips, kids, marriage, recipes, and current events.

Working women often have more in common with men, but even they have different favorite topics. Similarly, at social events, it's quite common for the men to talk to other men while the women talk to other women.

Why? Simply put, men and women enjoy talking about different things.

> According to the Talmud, women are more loquacious than men.[5] There are also gender differences in the type of talk. Men tend to be more concrete and offer advice and solutions to problems. Women tend to talk for emotional bonding.
>
> There is a cartoon strip where the wife calls to tell the husband that her car broke down and could he please come and help her.
>
> A few moments later, the husband calls back. "There's a tow truck on the way."
>
> The wife remarks, "I'm looking for sympathy, and he's giving me solutions."
>
> When women present problems, they want to be understood

---

5. Talmud, *Kiddushin* 49b.

and share their feelings, whereas men want to suggest how to solve problems. This may cause a communication problem, if, instead of empathizing with his wife, the husband suggests a solution. The wife may become upset that her feelings were not appreciated.[6]

When married couples have children, the kids take up a great amount of the conversation. The reason is obvious. This is a topic that both husbands and wives enjoy talking about. But when it comes to other topics, their interests are very different and that's where the problem lies.

Plugging In — and Tuning Out

WHILE WE'RE ON THE topic of communication, or the lack thereof, one of the biggest culprits is technology. BlackBerries and iPhones rob people of the little time that the family might spend together.

In the past, the wife would have wanted to spend time with her husband after dinner. Today she has an alternative. She can text her friends. Between the phone and the texting, it's easy for a husband to feel that his wife is more committed to everyone else but him. If you care about the relationships in your life, keep these gadgets far away from your sacred family time.

If technology presents a challenge to marriages, so can the passage of time. Over the years, interests begin to shift. Couples begin drifting apart. In the search for personal fulfillment, they acquire new hobbies. Some spouses may become more religious. When that happens, the other spouse feels this newfound religion as competition. This feeling intensifies when the religious spouse begins to insist that the other one get more involved.

---

6. Rabbi Dr. Abraham J. Twerski, *The First Year of Marriage* (Shaar Press, 2004), p. 119.

Getting involved in religion is wonderful, but it's important to be very sensitive to the feelings of the spouse. What is obvious and valuable to you may not be as obvious or valuable to your other half. To avoid conflict, don't isolate or ignore your spouse. The truth is, we can't become truly close to G-d if we tread on the feelings and sensitivities of others.

> Men enjoy different activities than women do.
> Wives are more dependent on their husbands for
> affection and wish to spend more time with them.

7 Important Words Men and Women Understand Differently

D ID YOU HEAR THE story about the couple who got married? The man knew he wanted to marry her from the first date, and spent the rest of their dates convincing her that she was the one. It's a common story. When men choose the woman they'll marry, their choice is based primarily on visual appeal. Many men have told me that after seeing their future spouse only once, they knew that she was the one they were going to marry.

"Honey, I love you with all my heart," the groom said to his new bride on their wedding night, "and unless that changes, I don't see any reason to bring it up again."

While men make snap decisions based on external attributes, women need more time.[1] For a woman to choose a partner, the potential mate needs to win over her heart.

---

1. In truth, the decision to marry (and certainly whom to marry) is not one that should be made hastily. Give yourselves some time to get to know each other and be sure of your decision.

This naturally requires time and patience, *and the process is a verbal one.* A woman needs to hear how much she is loved. It's the oxygen of her self-esteem.

I Just Called to Say "I Love You"

For a wife to believe that her husband cherishes her, she must hear the words "I love you" from him every single day. At first she may say that she doesn't believe him, but this is usually because she loves hearing the words so much that she wants him to say them again. Or it could be that he insulted her or hurt her feelings in some way, and the thought that he doesn't love her is embedded in her heart. In any event, he should repeat it to her every day, at every appropriate opportunity. He should also look for other words of affection, love, and warmth to tell her, too.[2]

It's very important for a woman to hear that her husband loves her. What about a man? Do men also crave to hear how much they are loved?

I would argue that while men like to hear that they are admired, respected, strong, and smart — anything that will boost the male ego — they don't have the same need to hear that they are loved.

It's not that men don't appreciate hearing it; it's just that the effect is different. When a man hears that he is loved, what he hears is, "You are a good husband." It's nice to hear these words, and they boost his ego, but they aren't necessary to his intrinsic self-worth. It is his wife's trust and respect that he needs more; if he knows that she relies on him and looks up to him, he feels valued.

---

2. Arush, *The Garden of Peace*, p. 274.

A woman, on the other hand, needs to know that she is loved for her worth. When a woman hears that she is loved, she hears, "You have value." The words reinforce her feeling that she has a good relationship. In her case, it's not an ego trip; it's essential to her self-esteem.

Most women need to hear this affirmation frequently, and the more often, the better. A woman who doesn't hear that she is loved starts to question herself. If this goes on for a couple of days she can go into a crisis. She becomes anxious, irritable, depressed. Her spouse, meanwhile, has no idea what's happening. All he knows is that his wife's personality has changed overnight.

More Than Lip Service

WHEN I SHARED THIS thought with an engaged couple, I noticed that the girl turned to stare at her future husband. When I asked her what she was thinking, she replied, "Mark won't say that he loves me. He just refuses!"

"Why aren't you willing to express your love for your future wife?" I asked Mark. "I assume that you love her. It would be a terrible idea to marry someone you don't love."

"That's exactly my point," he replied. "If I didn't love her, I wouldn't be marrying her. So why do I need to keep repeating the obvious?"

I shook my head. "You are making a mistake. You're making assumptions from your own perspective. You might not need to hear it, but women definitely need to hear these words, and often. Even if you don't feel such a strong emotion now, what does it hurt to say the words if it makes such a difference to your fiancée?"

Mark, like many men, could not relate to this point. On one level, Mark was right: The fact that a person is engaged or married demonstrates a level of love and commitment. Why does it make a difference if you say it or not? It doesn't make it any truer.

While this sounds logical to men, it sounds boorish and insensitive to women. How do we explain this seemingly irrational need for women to hear the words?

The answer goes back to the P's and the A's. Prestige, Power, and Pleasure do not necessarily require any words. But Affection does. So although a man does not need to hear professions of love to boost his self-esteem, the fact is that a woman does need them. This is why marriage is so challenging — even in something so basic, men and women are completely different.

If this is important to your spouse, say it. Better yet, say it with feeling. Don't deprive your spouse of something that fills her with energy and life.

I once asked a group that I was teaching why they thought that women need to hear that they are loved and valued.

A man said, "Men are more secure."

"That's not true," a woman responded. "Women can be very secure and strong."

"Let's go back to the A for Affection," I said. "When women feel connected to their husbands, it bolsters their own self-esteem. This doesn't imply that women are weaker. It's just part of their makeup."

Although men don't need to hear that they are loved as much as women do, they also need verbal reassurance. The fact is, men don't appreciate being taken for granted. Rather than hearing "I love you," they want to know that "you give me security" or, "I feel that I can always rely on you," or, "that was a smart maneuver."

Just as saying "I love you" feeds a woman's need for affection, hearing that their wives depend on them and respect them fortifies men's prestige and sense of power, which feeds their self-esteem.

The Power of a Word

On a trip to Israel, the passenger next to me said, "I received a text message from my daughter. It read, 'Dad I love you.' So I wrote back, 'How much?'

"She wrote, 'Very much.'

"That wasn't what I meant.

"I wrote back, 'That's very nice. What I meant is HOW MUCH is this text going to cost me?'"

Given that men and women have gender-specific needs, it should come as no surprise that the words "I love you" mean different things to men and women. A woman literally hears that she is loved. The man hears, "I am doing my job. I can expect to receive pleasure." On a deeper level he hears, "I have faults, but my wife still accepts me." This is a great self-esteem booster.

Words themselves are only a conduit for information. Real communication happens after the one hearing the words interprets their meaning. If I say "I love you" in Latin, you might not know what I'm saying, much less sense the emotion behind the expression. The listener filters the words through his experiences and perceptions, and formulates a conclusion. The words by themselves do not convey the message if the listener can't understand them.

When I communicate a feeling through words, I am allowing the other person to decide whether or not to connect to me. It becomes his choice how to decipher my words. I am just opening a door. The rest depends on him. If a person who is depressed is told, "I love you," this may mean very little to him. The word "love" doesn't generate any feeling as long as the person refuses (or is unable) to accept the message.

Since the words "I love you" don't convey the same message to men as they do for women, men don't realize the importance of hearing these words for women. That is why it is important for men to understand that a woman needs to hear the words to fulfill her need for Affection. Nothing else will do. For her, his saying "I love you" tells her, "I want a relationship with you; I want to connect." When a woman hears from her husband that she is loved, she feels cherished, and then she, in turn, wants to give him what he needs to be happy in the relationship.[3]

Contemplating this idea, it occurred to me that the Torah teaches us this lesson again and again. For example, the Torah states that the Jews were counted a number of times via a census.[4] Rashi[5] points out that G-d did not require a physical count to know how many Jews there were. Certainly He knew their number. Rather, the count was done to confirm *how important and cherished each person was*. When people value things, they review them often. Likewise, a woman can never hear "I love you" enough from her husband.

_____

3. The fact that speech is a special vehicle for connection goes all the way back to the time of Creation. The Psalmist says that the world was created through G-d's speech (Psalms 33:6). This idea is stated explicitly at the beginning of Genesis, "G-d *said*, 'There shall be light,' and there was light" (Genesis 1:3). This indicates that speech is a means to create. But we are told that G-d is indescribable and has no corporeal image or physical dimension, so what does it mean that "G-d said"? The Rambam states, "The Torah speaks in the language of men" (*Hilchot Mada* 1:9). Even though G-d has no mouth, the Torah uses common expressions so that we can relate to what G-d did. If that is the case, why does the Torah say that G-d created specifically through speech and not thoughts? According to Chassidic texts, there is a reason that the analogy of speech is used. Only if I wish to communicate with someone else do I need to speak. The Torah's declaration that "G-d said" is telling us that G-d made place for another existence. Before Creation, He was the only reality. Nothing existed but His Divine Presence. The act of creation required that G-d make "room" for another existence. In order for the world to appear "independent," G-d had to hide His Presence. But G-d used speech as a channel for us to relate to Him. Let us learn from G-d. He gives us our space, but conveys His interest in having a relationship with humanity. We, too, need to give our spouse their liberty, and at the same time, give them the words that make them open to reciprocating in the relationship.

4. Numbers 1:1.

5. Rabbi Shlomo Yitzchaki (1040–1105), famous commentator on the Bible and Talmud.

How We Respond to Arguments

WE WILL ADDRESS THE topic of arguments and conflict later in this book,[6] but for the sake of highlighting the differences between the way men and women react to conflict, I'll touch upon it here briefly.

What happens when men and women argue? Both men and women become anxious when they are criticized. But each reacts in different ways.

For the man, his ego is on the line. He thinks, *How dare my wife speak to me this way? Here I am, trying to be the best husband I can be, yet it's not good enough!*

Meanwhile, the woman feels like her self-esteem is being shattered. She thinks, *My husband shouted and insulted me. I can't believe this is happening. Our relationship is falling to pieces. My marriage (and maybe even my life) is depressing.*

Here, again, we see how the P's and A's play a role. The man, to whom Prestige is so important, sees criticism as an attack on his ego. For the woman, who needs Affection, criticism is a blow to the relationship, to her emotional connection with her husband.

For men, handling conflict in marriage can be extremely challenging. They are used to winning arguments and controlling situations. They often view arguments in terms of a competition. When a man feels that his wife is contradicting him, he takes it as a direct blow to his ego, so his knee-jerk reaction is to retrieve the reins by attacking, bickering, raising his voice, and even getting angry. A woman finds these tactics extremely intimidating. It might get her to surrender, but ultimately it will damage the relationship.

Women generally are not looking for control, but they also despise being manipulated and controlled by their spouse. When

---

6. See Part 3, "The Art of Communication."

a wife feels that her opinion doesn't count, she gets frustrated and depressed. *How can it be that I have no say in my own home? I accept that my husband is entitled to his opinion, but why must I always give in?* This triggers feelings of inadequacy and loneliness. She feels that her husband doesn't care about her and this affects her self-esteem.

When we talk about the beauty of marriage, we are referring to emotional satisfaction. Feeling loved in a relationship means that someone accepts me for who I am — the good and the bad. This is an extremely powerful feeling. This is also the reason that a marriage can be very painful. The person who can affirm your sense of self-worth can also damage it like no one else. If some stranger on the road insults you, chances are you'll get over it quickly. If a friend insults you, the hurt is much deeper. If your spouse hurts you, the pain can eventually destroy a marriage. We are much more open, and therefore vulnerable, to the person with whom we have a close relationship.

Proverbs states that "life and death depend on the tongue."[7] In this context, it means that words can be more painful than bullets or as invigorating as winning a gold medal. Telling your wife, "I love you," or saying to your husband, "I respect what you do for me," is the easiest thing in the world — and it can make such a difference to your marriage.

Women need to hear verbal affirmation more than men, but men also need to hear that their wives respect them.

---

7. Proverbs 18:21.

8 Love Is Not an Accident

THE STORY IS TOLD about the fisherman who caught a forty-pound salmon. "My master will be very happy — he loves salmon!" he exclaimed.

When the salmon heard how much the fisherman's master loved the fish, he thought, *Good. Soon I'll be back in the water.*

The fisherman brought the fish to the mansion where his master lived. When the fish was carried past the first gate, the security guard said, "Our master loves salmon."

The fisherman knocked on the door. Upon seeing the catch, the butler said, "Our master loves salmon!"

When the cook saw what the fisherman had brought, she grew excited and proclaimed, "Terrific! Our master loves salmon."

As the cook lifted up the plank of wood to slam down on the salmon, the fish screamed, "IF THE MASTER LOVES ME SO MUCH, WHY ARE YOU KILLING ME?"

To a certain extent, we all live this story. Our love is defined by what we're getting from the other person. The benefits may be physical, emotional, or spiritual, but the common denominator is that we have a personal interest. Let's face it: Does anyone marry a person he or she doesn't like? We choose to marry only people we believe will give us something, whether it's joy, satisfaction, companionship, stability, security, or love.

I Love You, but I Love Me More

THIS IS THE MODERN idea of marriage: I am willing to love you only as long as I get what I need. Obviously this is not true of everyone, but most people come to a relationship with the attitude of, "What can the other person do for me?" rather than, "What can I give to the other person?" They expect to be able to pursue their needs and lifestyle without considering the other person's needs. Since men and women are so different, how can such a marriage function? The answer is: It won't. It will probably fail unless both parties are aware of what it really means to be in a relationship.

> Why aren't marriages working out? It is because he (or she) is already in a relationship. Before one considers marriage, a person needs to become divorced from himself.[1]

I received a call one day from a newly wedded bride.

"Rabbi, I'm devastated," she said. "You won't believe this. We just got married and already we're in trouble. Our courtship was great. He was so courteous, a real mensch. When we had to choose a place to eat, he would say, 'Wherever you want.' What movie should we go to? 'You decide.' It was like a dream. Then, right after the wedding, he told me, 'My dear wife, in life we need to be fair. In our home I believe we should have equality.'

"'I fully agree,' I replied.

"'Do you recall that last year before we got married, we did everything your way?'"

"'Yes, of course I do.'

"'Great! This year it's my turn. Now we do everything my way.'"

At first, I was shocked. I couldn't believe what this young

---

1. Overheard from Rabbi Manis Friedman, author of *Doesn't Anyone Blush Anymore?* and dean of Bais Chanah in Minnesota.

woman had told me. But then it dawned on me: We all display this behavior at times. We all expect to be rewarded for our actions. We all feel that we deserve to receive the same amount of effort we put into the relationship.

In other words, all of us, to one extent or another, keep accounts. As long as the returns are equal to or higher than the investment, we are willing to hold on. The moment we feel that the venture is not "profitable," we begin evaluating whether we can improve the "bottom line." [2]

The fact that we are plagued with selfishness was brought home to me one summer. My wife and I take a group of kids for camp to California every year. One day, I was in the lobby of a hotel, and a man in his seventies approached me and remarked, "I like those tzitzit."[3]

I realized the man must be Jewish and wanted to encourage his interest. "If you want, I can get you a pair of tefillin[4] to don."

---

2. In this vein, the Talmud states, "In the West, they would ask a lad who was engaged to be married, '*Matza* or *motze*?'" (*Berachot* 8a). These two words refer to two statements of King Solomon. The first is from Proverbs: "*Matza ishah matza tov* — One who has found a wife has found goodness" (Proverbs 18:22) — i.e., marriage is a good experience. The second is from Ecclesiastes (7:26): "*Motze ani mar mimavet et ha'ishah* — I have discovered something that is more bitter than death: the wife…" The Sages would ask a groom before he married, "Is she a good catch or one who will eventually disappoint you?" How could the prospective groom answer this question? If the marriage didn't look good from the beginning, he wouldn't be getting married in the first place. The question the Rabbis were posing was, "What are your motives? Is there a sincere commitment or do you have vested interests? Are you focused on what's in it for you? Or are you focused on how to become a good spouse?" When you are focused on making your partner happy, it's good (*matza tov*). When you are focused on your own needs, the relationship ultimately will become more bitter than death (*ha'ishah mar mimavet*).

3. A garment with fringes that Jewish men wear to remind them of the commandments.

4. Phylactery boxes that contain biblical texts, which men are commanded to don daily.

The man refused my offer. "I don't believe in religion," he said. "All wars have been started for religious reasons."

His reply got me thinking. *Wow, how many wars were initiated because of religion?* I brought up the topic a few days later with some friends. One of them pointed out, "The Second World War did not start out as a religious war. Look at Stalin. He killed millions of his own people because he was a Communist who believed in government, not G-d."

> A single woman once confided to her male friend, "I've gone out with so many men, but I feel like they're only interested in my dad's money. You can't imagine how much I would give to find someone who is really interested in me."
> The friend replied, "How much?"

I came to realize that, despite what people claim, almost all wars begin for the same reason — selfishness. An egomaniac wants control, so he sets out to conquer and rule. Some may have used religion to justify their cause, but the underlying reason is simply to gain power and wealth.

Marriage is not a war, but if people enter it simply for what they can gain, it will almost certainly become one. As long as you are concerned about "how will I benefit from this relationship?" it's doomed to failure. It will lead only to fruitless discussions, arguments, and discontent.

What Has Changed?

OVER FIFTY YEARS AGO the world was different. In the old days, it was accepted that the man had the first and last word — and it wasn't "Yes, dear." The woman knew who had the authority in the marriage (it was very clear "who wore the pants in the house"), and this was not challenged. We might look back at those times and think that those were idyllic days. Divorce was less common and couples almost certainly had fewer arguments.

Even today, in certain countries and cultures, this is still the norm. In those cultures, being submissive is one of the conditions that women accept with the wedding ring. We who live in a Western culture find it hard to identify with such a marriage. It's hard for us to believe a woman could be happy with this system. And the truth is, although this arrangement reduces the likelihood of quarrels and conflict, it also doesn't permit the woman to achieve true satisfaction and fulfillment in her relationship. While feeling loved raises a woman's self-esteem, being controlled and manipulated hurts her self-esteem.

There is no doubt that the number of divorces in the Western world is far greater than in cultures that maintain the old system. But this does not mean that their marriages are better or happier. It indicates only that women are less independent. It may also be that they are afraid of getting divorced, usually because they have no means of supporting themselves.

Regardless of how it used to be and still is in some places, the world has changed. Women have more rights and expect to be treated equally. They refuse, and rightfully so, to be controlled or treated like an inferior by a spouse.

But this does have its downside. Today many women try to prove that they are equal. They become defensive and highly sensitive when their spouses disagree with them. The result is more confrontations, especially if the man tries to run his marriage with an "I am the boss" attitude. Unquestionably, this is one of the causes of the skyrocketing divorce rate today.

Why Do I Love You?

THE SAGES IN *PIRKEI AVOT* teach us, "There are two kinds of love. One type depends on external factors [such as beauty]. As long as the external characteristic exists, this love will exist. Once it evaporates, so does the love."[5]

The second type does not depend on external attributes. It does not depend on any one thing. Since it doesn't depend on anything, it lasts forever. According to *Pirkei Avot*, the love between Amnon and Tamar was based on superficial infatuation, so it wasn't a true and everlasting love. The brotherly love between David and Yonatan was unconditional and, therefore, unshakable.[6]

Let's give another example. A couple starts dating. He showers her with attention, gives her gifts, and makes her feel like she is at the top of the world. She is very pretty and always dresses well. He is proud to be seen with her. They fall in love and get married. A child comes along, and they couldn't be happier.

Then he begins to spend more time at the office. After all, now he has a family to support. When he comes home, all he wants to do is relax. Instead he is faced with a wife who is needy and demanding. She is less concerned about her looks than before. She doesn't dress up like she used to. She is kept up every night by the baby and is constantly tired and stressed. At the end of the day, after spending all her time with the baby, she is eager for adult company. She looks forward to her husband coming home and anticipates the gifts he will bring her like he used to in the past. But not only are there no gifts, he doesn't seem interested in spending that much time with her.

Their dissatisfaction grows. The reasons they got married are no longer there. He doesn't give her gifts anymore, and she doesn't take care of her appearance. They don't realize that their

---

5. Mishnah, *Avot* 5:19.

6. Ibid. Amnon and Tamar were both children of King David. Amnon was infatuated with Tamar and eventually coerced her into having physical relations with him.

love was based on superficial things, and now that those things are gone, their love fades. All they think is, *Where has the spark gone? What happened to the person I married?*[7]

Or take the case of the woman who is engaged to a man who is articulate and persuasive. She is fascinated by how he can talk his way out of any problem, at his capacity to convince others that his opinions are the right ones. It's not surprising that he uses this talent to make her feel special and cherished. What happens when they get married and the wife begins to sense that her husband is nothing more than a smooth talker? That he isn't truly sincere and can lie without skipping a beat? She begins to realize that the part of him that attracted her is superficial and empty. She no longer feels any love for him, let alone respect.

Everyone needs to be loved. This is absolutely essential for a stable and happy marriage. But many people misconstrue the true meaning of love. It's universally understood that love is an emotion toward another person or creature. It is a powerful emotion, one that can empower people to do extraordinary feats such as lifting a car to save one's child.

But love can also be a very selfish feeling. If I love someone,

---

7. This is not to say that a husband shouldn't give his wife gifts, or that a wife shouldn't try to look nice for her husband. But this should not be the whole basis of their love for each other. The Torah teaches, "When you go out to war against your enemies... and you see among the captives a woman who is very attractive and you desire her... you may bring her back to your house... You shall let her mourn her family for a full month [without beautifying herself]. Then [if you still desire], you can marry her" (Deuteronomy 21:10–13). According to Rashi, G-d realized that a man could lose self-control when he sees an attractive woman during a time of battle. Rather than permit him to follow his desires, the Torah commands him to take her home. Furthermore, she is forbidden to beautify herself during the time that she lives in his house. The Torah expects that at some point the soldier will come to his senses and send her back — especially when he sees beneath whatever surface beauty she had. In both cases, the message is the same: In a lasting relationship, there must be more than just the immediate gratification of one's physical needs. There must be give-and-take.

but my love is based on what the other person can do for me rather than what I can give to him, then that love is a completely selfish love. You don't really love the other person; you love only yourself. This is one of the key reasons that marriages fail. People are not truly committing themselves to each other. The relationship is about what they can get — whether it's status, pleasure, or money — and once that element is gone, they no longer have any reason to be in the relationship.[8]

Sometimes you find couples who say that if it weren't for their children, they would end their union. That's sad. It confirms that these marriages are not functioning, that they are bound together by an external element. The glue of a working relationship is true love. When the glue becomes the kids, it's not a relationship.

In the light of what we now know about the P's and the A's, we can understand why marriages turn bitter. A man seeks Prestige, Pleasure, and Power for his self-esteem. A woman seeks Affection, Appearance, and Accomplishment to feel good. It

---

8. This concept can be understood from a biblical law. The Torah states that when a person builds a new home, he must put up a guardrail to prevent someone from falling from the roof (Deuteronomy 22:8). If this was not done and someone falls, the homeowner is guilty of bloodshed. The verse that states this law uses a strange expression, "The fallen one shall fall." The verse should have stated, "The person shall fall." Why call the person "fallen" before he falls? Also, this rule of putting up a guardrail also applies to an old home that was purchased. Why then does the Torah state, "When you build a new home..."? The Lubavitcher Rebbe, *zy'a*, explains that this verse is referring to marriage. When you build a new home — i.e., when you get married — you need to put up a fence. Take measures to protect the sanctity of your relationship and marriage. Using this idea, we can reinterpret the words from the same verse, "*V'lo tasim damim b'veitecha.*" The words literally mean, "Do not spill blood in your home." But the word *damim* can also mean "money." The verse is hinting that one should make sure that money is not the foundation of one's home. Don't get married for material benefits. Why? "For the fallen one shall fall" — someone who marries for money has already fallen. Such a person does not understand the important values of life. If he or she marries for material gain, or some other personal interest, then "the fallen shall continue to fall."

follows that they will seek these things in their marriage. In our example above of the couple who married for external reasons, the man felt that marrying a woman who dresses well and appreciates him contributed to his Prestige. The woman enjoyed the gifts and attention he showered on her, feeding her need for Affection. When these things disappeared, their love for each other disappeared. They no longer felt they were gaining anything from the marriage.

Does this mean that if we truly love our spouse, we should never expect to benefit from them?

Of course not. In every relationship there are things we give to each other and there are things we receive. But if I need to receive more than I desire to give — if the only reason that I am in the relationship is because of what I will get out of it — the relationship will inevitably fall apart.

> Conditional, selfish love dissipates when its conditions are not met, but unconditional, selfless love is constant and eternal. Conditional love all too often means the obliteration or subjection of one individual; instead of two becoming one, the love of the more dominant person consumes the other. Unconditional love, though, the love of transcendence, enables you to put aside your selfish desires and love that person accordingly.[9]

A couple went to a priest to get married. During the interview, the priest asked, "Would you like the traditional or the modern ceremony?"

"What's the difference?" they asked.

"In the traditional ceremony, the bride and groom each

---

9. Rabbi Simon Jacobson, *Toward a Meaningful Life: The Wisdom of the Rebbe* (Morrow Publishers, 1995), p. 61.

light a candle and blow them out. The modern style is for each person to light a candle and leave it lit."

"How does a burning candle make a ceremony more modern?"

"The lit candle represents individuality and personality — the ego. By blowing out your candles, each of you demonstrates a willingness to nullify your desires to those of your spouse. Furthermore, both spouses commit themselves to the marriage under any condition. Today, people aren't willing to relinquish their needs for their spouse. What would you prefer?"

The groom thought for a moment and said, "How about if we both light the candles and the bride blows hers out."

Selfish love is temporary. If love is dependent on something — looks, money, or a charismatic personality — and that something is taken away, the love fades.

PART 2

It's Not about Me, It's about You

9 The Marriage Pyramid

ALL MARRIAGES DISSOLVE AND terminate for the same reason. Can you guess what it is? The answer is: The love has disappeared.

This commonly happens when the love is based on externals — the selfish love we talked about in the previous chapter. When those things disappear, the love often disappears. When people cease to love each other, they are prone to divorce. One might add that emotionally, they are already divorced. It might take some time to get a physical divorce or they might even decide to stay together, but on the emotional level their relationship has already terminated.

It makes sense to say that love is the glue that holds a marriage together. But we should not ignore the importance of commitment for a long-lasting relationship. Love is the life force, while commitment can be compared to the brain waves. As long

> A man died, and his wife passed away soon after. When she reached heaven and saw her spouse, she cried out, "My dear husband, we are reunited!"
> "Excuse me," he replied. "Didn't we agree that we were married 'until death do us part'?"

as the brain waves are functioning, you can survive, but without the heart pumping blood efficiently, life will be restricted. Love is what maintains the connection, and if it is lacking, the bond will end.

Some people might argue that other elements destroy marriage: troubled finances or lack of communication, for example. Although these things are important for the well-being of the marriage, the reason the marriage suffers is because troubled finances and lack of communication erode the union of the couple. If the couple's love for each other isn't strong enough, then the bond breaks. On the other hand, if a couple truly loves each other, they can weather any difficulties they face. They will make an effort to work on their communication and overcome the challenges of their differences.

For this reason, love sits on top of the pyramid. It is, indeed, the glue that holds the relationship together.

> A couple was on the verge of ending their union after a very short time together. After a brief attempt to reconcile, the couple went to their rabbi to see what could be done.
>
> "What has brought you to the point that you are at now, where you are not able to keep this marriage together?" the rabbi asked.
>
> "In the seven weeks that we've been together," the husband said, "we haven't been able to agree on one thing."
>
> "Eight weeks," the wife said.

When the Bond Breaks

IT'S SAFE TO SAY that when a couple marries, they most probably love each other. If love is the bond that keeps them together, what happened? Why did the marriage deteriorate?

No matter how much they love each other, eventually they are going to have a conflict. Whether it is due to a misunderstanding or cultural differences or upbringing, all couples fight. When a couple argues too often, this begins to eat away at the core of their relationship.

It's difficult to love a person who fights with you all the time. It takes a toll on the love and eventually on the marriage. On the other hand, if there is little interaction, this also diminishes the feelings that one spouse has for the other.

Why do couples experience conflicts?

Generally, each spouse thinks that he or she is fulfilling his or her responsibilities. When they feel they are being attacked, either directly with criticism or indirectly with sarcasm, they become irritated, anxious, and defensive. They feel there is no justification for this behavior; after all, they did nothing wrong. They are fulfilling their side of the relationship, so why is the other person complaining and acting hostile?

People who feel attacked tend to react aggressively. This can also be triggered when a spouse feels ignored and taken for granted. Naturally, the spouse will express feelings of discontent and generate negative vibes. This inevitably evolves into a discussion where each side tries to convince the other that he or she is correct, with both of them feeling that they are the victim of an irrational spouse. Eventually each party concludes that their partner is inflexible, stubborn, or just plain obnoxious.

With this type of thinking, you can imagine that the conflicts will not decrease but, on the contrary, only increase.

Everything could be solved if the couple would, instead of arguing, sit down and discuss their issues calmly and rationally, couldn't it? In a perfect world, each party articulates his or her needs and works out a mutually beneficial solution to every issue. Why is it so difficult for a husband and wife to share and communicate?

It's because men and women don't see eye to eye on many issues. Their perspectives are distinctive and unique. Understanding the differences between men and women will help them resolve the underlying issues.

We described these differences between men and women in the first chapters of this book. These differences manifest themselves on many levels: physiological, emotional, and spiritual. Specifically, women pursue Affection, Appearance, and Achievement for their self-esteem, and men pursue Power, Pleasure, and Prestige. We also saw that these differences greatly affect marital harmony. Add to this mixture economic strains, health problems, family conflicts, and emotional balances, which serve only to intensify the conflict, and you have a recipe for disaster.

In simple words, men and women seek different things to boost their self-esteem. Therefore, they don't see things the same way and have different priorities. This difference creates a level of anxiety and a lot of misunderstandings. It's no surprise that they end up arguing and fighting. This can cause the relationship to deteriorate, breaking the bond of love between them and ending in divorce.

So even though love is at the top of the pyramid, unless we deal with the bottom of the pyramid — our need to pursue the P's and the A's, and how to help our spouse achieve these needs — the entire structure will come tumbling down.

The Bottom of the Pyramid

BASED ON THIS EVALUATION, we can appreciate why it is incumbent on each individual to evaluate and understand the things that boost self-esteem. Then the couple can figure out how to balance these needs to properly nourish the relationship. Once couples strengthen their respective visions of self-esteem, they can resolve any differences that divide them and begin to focus on their spouse's needs. Instead of focusing on "me," I begin to focus on "you."

By focusing on each other, the couple can continually improve their relationship and enjoy a marriage that is fulfilling in every possible way. In this way, they will strengthen their bond and deepen their connection.

That connection is based on love, but now we can redefine the word "love," not as a selfish feeling, where we focus on getting what we want, but rather as a deeper love. The kind of love that maintains the connection between the couple — that forms the glue that holds the marriage together — is unconditional love. This is achieved through *commitment*. When we are committed to developing a strong relationship, then we are willing to give to our spouse unconditionally.

Once the marriage is consummated, we need to change our perspective. It's not about me anymore; rather, it's about my spouse. Or, better yet, my spouse is me; what is in his or her interest is in my interest.

So from conditional love, which is often the basis of relationships at the beginning, we begin to entertain the idea of unconditional love. The relationship must evolve: Selfish love must transition into true, selfless love.

This transformation requires commitment: commitment to focusing on the other person's needs and not just my own, commitment to making the marriage strong, commitment to sticking with it even when things get tough.

It's All about the Commitment

IN THE PAST, THE concept of marriage meant more than a convenient relationship; it meant a commitment. Two people who decided to marry undertook to make the relationship work in all circumstances — in other words, I may have chosen to marry for selfish reasons, but my commitment to my spouse is eternal.

Once when I paid a *shivah* visit to comfort a mourner, the

mourner was telling me about her deceased mother and I asked about her parents' marriage. She replied that it was very good. I went into a whole treatise on the many benefits of a good marriage — the stability it gives to future generations, the respect and positive environment that it creates in the home, and so on.

When I finished, the woman said, "No, Rabbi, you don't get it. They fought all the time, but they loved each other."

Now, that's commitment. Today they probably would have divorced. But in those days, they were in it for the long haul.

> An elderly couple came to the rabbi to ask for a divorce. The husband was in his late nineties and the wife was trailing close behind.
>
> Rabbi: "Excuse me, why do you want to get divorced?"
> Couple: "We're fighting too much."
> Rabbi: "When did this begin?"
> Couple: "About seventy years ago."
> Rabbi (surprised): "Why did you wait so long?"
> Couple: "We were waiting for the kids to die."

Full Commitment Does Not Have to Mean 24/7

THIS SOUNDS IMPOSSIBLE TO achieve. How is it possible to be 100 percent giving and selfless to another person 100 percent of the time? For years, scientists debated the question of whether the earth or the sun is the center of the universe.[10] Which is it? Neither. "I" am the center. Most human beings live as if they are

---

10. The Lubavitcher Rebbe, *zy'a*, explains how the earth can be the center even according to science. (*Mind over Matter: The Lubavitcher Rebbe on Science, Technology and Medicine* [Shamir, 2003], p. 75).

the center of the universe. Needless to say, this doesn't make for a very successful marriage.

Intellectually it makes sense that being selfish causes most marital conflicts, and that a good marriage requires a full commitment to each other. But emotionally, this is almost impossible to achieve. How can I truly feel that someone else is more important to me than I am myself?

At times we can achieve this feeling with our children, but that's really because we see them as an extension of ourselves. We have a harder time seeing our spouses that way. The bonds between spouses and between parents and children are both based on love. But the love we feel toward our children is unconditional. We don't divorce children; parents and children can fall out and argue, but the essential connection remains. When it comes to your spouse, however, it's hard to be completely selfless all the time.

I was once invited to the beach house of one of my congregants. I met his father there, an intellectual person, very well-read, a respected lawyer, and an honorable statesman. During our conversation he told me that the previous year, he had begun to don tefillin, but had recently stopped.

"Why?" I asked.

"Well, in the prayers it says you should love G-d with all your heart, soul, and might. But love is something I feel for my wife. I don't feel that I can truly love G-d like I love my spouse. I feel like a hypocrite."

"Dear Moshe," I said, "I am impressed by your sincerity, but let me ask you a question. Do you actually love your wife 24/7 with the same intensity? Of course not. In a relationship there are different moments. The feelings you have for your wife fluctuate according to the circumstances.

"So too with G-d. It goes without saying that we don't have an intense conscious love for G-d all the time. However, if you can feel a connection at certain moments, then this confirms that you have a relationship with Him. So saying that you should love G-d with all your heart, soul, and might is not just lip service."

> The Alter Rebbe told his son, Rav Dov Ber, to touch his hand. He asked, "What do you feel?"
> "I feel a hand."
> The Alter Rebbe said, "When you touch with a hand, you feel the hand. When you touch with the heart, you feel the soul."

It's true: It is extremely difficult to feel completely selfless toward your spouse all the time. It is impossible to expect a person to love unconditionally all the time. It's not even necessarily the right thing to do: In order to function, you also need to be able to have your needs fulfilled. However, if you come to your relationship with the right mindset — that a marriage is about giving, not just getting — you will experience moments of intense, unconditional love toward your spouse and the marriage will flourish.

Couples divorce when the love has disappeared. This happens when the couple argues constantly over their differences, rather than being committed to understanding and resolving them.

10 The First Step: A New Mindset

ONE EVENING, A SYNAGOGUE member called me. "Rabbi, my father is in terrible shape! The doctor said that two of his arteries that bring blood to the brain are clogged. He is sure my father won't survive the night."

I went over to their home immediately to say a prayer and be with the family in their moment of need. The following day, I didn't hear from the family so I called the son, expecting the worst.

"How are things doing?" I asked.

"Everything is fine," the son announced.

"Wow, a miracle!" I proclaimed.

"According to the doctor, the arteries have been clogged for a number of years," the son told me.

"So how did he survive?" I wondered.

"It's unbelievable. The body found new channels to bring the blood to the brain."

You Don't Have to Learn to Live with It

MAINTAINING A HEALTHY DIET by eating whole grains and vegetables and avoiding alcohol and soda is better for your body.

Regardless, there are people who manage to stay alive and even claim to feel good partaking of fatty foods, fried foods, sugary beverages, and excess alcohol. Just as the body adjusts to manage the toxins that are introduced to it from a poor diet, or creates new channels to send blood flowing to the brain when arteries are clogged, people adjust emotionally even if they're not getting what they need from their marriage.

I might not enjoy cold winters, but if I live in Canada, this is my reality and I must learn how to manage.

But what is more ideal? A body that's managing the toxins it is being fed or a body that's thriving on a healthy diet?

Many couples find themselves settling for their present situation *because they don't realize it could be any different.* They think that this is marriage and don't realize that they are only surviving when they could be thriving. Perhaps they are conscious of an underlying dissatisfaction, but they don't really know why they are dissatisfied. If the husband spends too much time away from home, or the wife acts very needy or disdainful, they just chalk it up to a normal part of marriage.

> **Never doubt your wife's decisions. Just look at who she married.**

Even if your marriage is functioning and you are happy, most people would agree that there is always room for improvement.

Either way, before you can improve, you must be able to understand what you need to do to improve. The first step, then, is to cultivate the right mindset. Your perception of your spouse and your marriage will affect how you treat each other.

Harry was very excited. He was finally getting married to the girl of his dreams. Right before his nuptials, he was on his way out of the office when his boss came over to him and said, "Congratulations, Harry! I just wanted to tell you that I've been married for thirty years, and I'm sure that you will always remember this day with the fondest of memories. It will be unforgettable!"

"But, sir," said Harry, "I'm not getting married until tomorrow."

"Yes, I know!"

Recognize That You Are Different

WITHOUT UNDERSTANDING THAT MEN and women are different, it will be difficult to make the right efforts to improve your marriage. Women should comprehend how they are wired and what boosts their own self-esteem. They should realize that their needs are very different from a man's.

In essence, women should realize that the way men behave is not something they choose or are even aware of. It's part of their nature. The woman's desire to be the center of her spouse's life is unnatural and unusual from a male perspective. Once women accept this reality, they will be able to assist their husbands in understanding their needs.

Similarly, men should not expect marriage to always be a smooth ride, even when they feel there's no reason for turbulence. An unhappy spouse generates stress. Once men learn that their wives' complaints are expressions of feeling emotionally distanced or not being taken into consideration, they can address their wives' anxiety and the accusations that result.

Recently I gave a talk to a group of men who were newly married. As I explained this idea to them, it was fascinating to see their expressions turn to relief. Each one had thought that he was the only one dealing with these issues. It was a revelation for them to realize that their struggles in marriage were normal.

For a relationship to function optimally, each spouse needs to first try to understand the other. *Realizing that each one needs very different things is the beginning of the road to a happy, fulfilling marriage.* This is where the P's and the A's come in. Generally women need to feel loved (Affection) in order to have healthy self-esteem. This is accomplished by giving them attention. A man, on the other hand, needs to feel respected and admired (Prestige). He needs to know that his wife trusts him and feels she can rely on him.

Someone I know used to arrive home from work at around seven-thirty. Occasionally he would come in at seven-forty-five and sometimes as late as eight o'clock. Whenever he arrived home after seven-thirty, his wife would get upset. Sometimes she complained. Sometimes she would greet him with a sour face. Either way, he was greeted by an unhappy wife.

"Why are you home late?" she would ask.

Husband: "I had things to do at the office. I wasn't just twiddling my thumbs. I had important things to take care of."

Wife: "But don't you realize that I'm here waiting for you?"

Husband: "That's nice, but sometimes things come up. I can't just drop everything."

Wife: "Then you need to call me and tell me you are running late."

He felt nagged. He thought his wife was being irrational. She felt that he was acting inconsiderate. The situation never got resolved.

What was really going on?

She was anxious to see her husband after an entire day, and expected that he was looking forward to seeing her, and that if for some reason he couldn't make it on time, he would call and tell her that he was going to be late. He, on the other hand, was not experiencing the same feeling of desperation to see his wife. It wasn't that he didn't love her, but it wasn't an essential need. Both of them felt they were the victims of a spouse who was indifferent to their needs and feelings.

The missing ingredient here was humility, the "unconditional love" factor rather than the "selfish love" factor. If they had been able to understand each other's nature, she wouldn't have felt so hurt and would not have overreacted. Instead of assuming that her husband meant to hurt her, she would have set aside her own ego and simply explained her needs in a calm way, and ultimately they would have been able to avoid unnecessary conflict.

He, on the other hand, needed to see that his wife only wanted to spend time with him after not seeing him all day. If he had been able to set aside the attack on his ego that he felt when she complained about his lateness, he would have been able to see through the accusations and realize she was just expressing this need. Although he did not have the same need to spend time with his wife, he would have made the effort anyway for her sake.

This is what women need to do to avoid feeling ignored or neglected. They must process the information differently. Instead of assuming that their husbands don't care enough to pay attention, they should envision a very focused, hardworking person who is trying to support the family. That's why he is preoccupied and does not dedicate as much time as he should to his wife. The responsibility of being the provider can be very stressful, and he takes this responsibility very seriously.

On the other hand, a man should be sensitive to his wife's emotional needs and realize that when he married, he committed himself to be a dedicated husband. But being a good husband does not only mean being a good provider; his wife also needs his attention, affection, and appreciation.

Years ago I recall reading about a husband and wife situation that was very perplexing. To resolve it, a rabbi was needed with the wisdom of King Solomon. Fortunately, the right rabbi was there.

Every summer, thousands of families relocate from New York City to the Catskill Mountains. The husbands work all week in the city and drive up to join the family for the weekends. On Sunday, they drive back to the city.

In this instance, the wife and husband were deeply divided about how to conduct their vacation home. The wife took total and sole responsibility for their kids the entire week. During the weekend, she felt she needed to rest and that it was up to her husband to take over. Her husband worked hard all week and rushed up to the Catskills on Friday. He needed his weekends to relax and unwind, which meant that his wife should watch the kids.

The rabbi considered both sides and then offered his opinion. "The husband should consider that his wife must be exhausted from taking care of the children the entire week by herself. He should look for ways to help her get a little rest. The wife should consider that her husband must be exhausted from working and commuting. She should look for ways to help him get a little rest. By taking this perspective, each will assist the other, and the marriage will continue to function."

Permit me to share a personal story.

One of the areas of contention in many marriages is the different driving styles of husbands and wives. I tend to drive on the fast track. While my driving skills are quite good, some people are uncomfortable with the way I drive. My wife claims that it makes her feel unsafe and nervous. "I get knots in my stomach from your driving," she says.

"Do you trust me?" I ask.

"Of course. This is not a trust issue. It's just how I feel."

She acknowledges that I am a good driver and have good reflexes when I need to maneuver out of hairy situations, but she still insists that I slow down. It goes without saying that I consider myself a safe driver. It's true that I'm a bit aggressive on the road, but this is not something that makes me feel nervous. Even when I slow down to honor my wife's request, I'm still driving faster than she would appreciate.

For a long time, I couldn't comprehend why she was so anxious. My attitude changed the day a shul member drove several other members and me to our local cemetery. The man was a good and experienced driver, but he habitually accelerated and then slowed abruptly whenever he approached other cars. His driving style made me nervous. I wasn't intellectually worried about his driving ability. I was emotionally tense (and not because we were headed to a cemetery). At that moment, it became clear to me what my wife had been trying to tell me: "I trust you, but I feel uneasy." Needless to say, I resolved to drive more slowly whenever my wife was in the car.

In this case, there were no quick fixes and immediate results — I still like to drive fast — but there was definitely a greater conscious effort to please my spouse. This happened only because I was able to see life from her perspective.

Love Needs to Be Nurtured

OUR SAGES TELL US, "One should be soft and flexible like a reed and not stiff and unyielding like a cedar."[1] For a marriage to succeed, both parties must overcome their egos and personal interests. They need to bend and not be inflexible. Plain and simple: Stop looking around all the time to see if you are getting everything you expected and envisioned from your marriage. Stop asking, "Am I getting all I bargained for? Do others get more than me? Did I get the best deal? Have I gained more now that I am married? Is my life as fulfilled as I hoped?"

If you really want to have a great marriage, you need to change the script. "Is *my spouse* getting what he or she is hoping

---

1. Talmud, *Taʾanis* 20.

for? Am I being a dedicated husband or wife? What else should I be doing to make my spouse's life better?"

> There is never a reason or justification for being so wrapped up in your own sense of self-importance that you exclude your family, your neighbors, your people, or your Creator from your mind, heart, and life.[2]

The Torah discusses the laws of the *sotah* (Numbers 5:12), a woman suspected of being unfaithful, right after it discusses the laws of bringing gifts to the *kohen* (priest). Why? According to Rashi, this teaches us that if a person doesn't bring the *kohen* the donations required by the Torah, he will end up going to the *kohen* anyway — with his wife whom he suspects of being a *sotah*. What is the connection?

A person who will not share his wealth with the *kohen* is selfish. If this person is self-centered with regard to the *kohen*, he is certainly selfish with regard to his wife. When a woman feels abandoned because her husband is focused only on his interests, she becomes more vulnerable to another man.

The Talmud says regarding a person who is haughty, "G-d proclaims, 'He and I can't live together!'"[3] Humility is Judaism's greatest virtue, as Ramban (Nachmanides) wrote to his son, "Humility is the greatest quality of all the fine attributes one can acquire."[4]

Without humility, it is impossible to have any kind of genuine relationship. Hillel the Elder taught, "Don't do to others what you wouldn't want done to you,"[5] and Rabbi Akiva taught that

---

2. Rabbi Manis Freidman, *Doesn't Anyone Blush Anymore?* (Harper Collins, 1990), p. 45.
3. Talmud, *Sotah* 5a.
4. *Iggeret HaRamban*, cited in *Meulefes Sapirim*.
5. Talmud, *Shabbat* 31a.

"Love your neighbor as yourself" is an important principle in the Torah.[6] What does it mean to love your neighbor as yourself? Just as you want people to provide for your needs, you should seek to please others. Needless to say, if this law applies to your neighbor, how much more does it apply to your spouse! Find out what his or her needs are and provide them.

If you can apply the law of "Love your fellow as yourself" to your spouse, he or she automatically receives the attention, affection, and love she craves and needs. But a person who is arrogant cannot do so; he is not able to step outside of himself in order to analyze what his spouse needs and then willingly give it to her.

Imagine that two people are pulling on a rope in different directions. Eventually, the rope will tear. This is precisely what happens in a relationship when each person is focused on his or her own ego and agenda.

There is, however, an important difference in our rope-relationship analogy that should be mentioned. The two people pulling the rope are clearly not willing to give an inch. But most of us realize that a marriage can't work if we seek only our own satisfaction. No relationship can survive a unilateral commitment. Few people will accept such terms. So we do give, we make concessions, we make compromises, we do things we would prefer to avoid because without this effort the marriage won't last. However, if one spouse invests only the bare minimum necessary for the marriage to function, the other will quickly perceive this pattern. The union may endure, but it certainly will not be psychologically or emotionally satisfying. On the contrary, it will probably stagnate and become monotonous.

Think about it. If my spouse has no genuine interest in me,

6. *Talmud Yerushalmi, Nedarim* 9:4.

my life, needs, concerns, worries, issues, and stresses, how can we have a real relationship? We can live together, go on vacations, attend social events, share some nice moments, but it is not an ideal marriage.

As long as the couple views themselves as two entities, each one seeking his or her own fulfillment, the marriage will not last. Marriage isn't a 50-50 proposition, it's 100-100. Each person must be fully committed to being there for the other person — 100 percent.

Let Your Spouse Know What You Really Want

NOT ONLY IS IT important to realize that your spouse has different needs, and therefore, you need to view his or her behavior differently — but also realize that *your spouse* may not be aware that *you* have different needs. What is clear to you may not be apparent at all to your spouse.

A member of my congregation once called me to relate that his wife kept complaining that they never go out at night.

"Honey, you are right," her husband said soothingly. "Why don't you plan an evening that we can go out? Just tell me when."

A couple of weeks went by and his wife again complained, "We still haven't gone out."

"Yes, that's true," her husband replied. "But we agreed that you were going to arrange it and tell me."

"Look," his wife said, "it's important for me to see that this is important to you, too. Why don't you take the initiative?"

A week later, the husband dutifully called his wife from work and said, "Let's go out tonight."

"Yes, that's a great idea," his wife enthusiastically replied.

After putting the children to sleep, the husband turned to his wife and said, "So, are you ready to go out?"

"Not really. I'm a little tired. But if you want, we can go out."

The husband was dumbfounded. "It doesn't make sense," he told me. "First, she says we never go out. I say I'm willing. She insists I should arrange it, and I do. Then we end up staying home!"

"My friend," I said to him, "you need to hear what your wife was telling you. Your wife was really saying, 'I don't feel that I am the priority in your life because we don't go out at night.' You found a solution. She wasn't looking for a solution. She was looking for some expression from you that you were thinking about her! When you arranged to go out, she declined because your arranging to go out confirmed that she was important in your eyes. After that, she didn't really need to leave the house."

Understanding that what is apparent to you may be inconceivable to your spouse will remove quite a bit of tension. When a woman begins getting anxious because she is being ignored, slighted, taken for granted, or criticized, she should think, *My husband does not intend to hurt my feelings. His communication skills are underdeveloped.* After the storm settles, she should communicate to her spouse what she feels took place, even though he was unaware of how she was feeling. By speaking to him calmly and honestly, she is much more likely to get a positive response from her husband, who will try to amend the state of affairs.

A man also needs to appreciate and comprehend that his wife is an entirely different type of person than he — that she is wired with greater emotional dependency and is sensitive when she feels that she is being taken for granted and is not a high priority in his life. Then, instead of going on the defensive when she is upset with him, or questions and criticizes his behavior, he can express empathy for her. With kind words and a little affection, he can resolve the issue with relatively little effort.

Keep Your Eye on the Ball

WHILE WE'RE TALKING ABOUT changing our perspective about marriage, here is something you may not have thought about: All the benefits of marriage — companionship, friendship, relations, children, and support — can be achieved without the institution of a formal marriage. So why get married?

In Jewish tradition, there is only one reason to get married: because G-d said so. Simply put, it's a commandment.[7]

Why is this an important mindset to be aware of?

If you choose to marry because it's optional and you think it's a nice idea, you also feel that you can just as easily change your mind when it doesn't feel so nice anymore. You've changed your mind; no problem — you'll get a divorce and get on with your life. But if your decision to marry is based on the goal of fulfilling G-d's plan, you need to determine whether *He* agrees that the relationship should end.[8]

The Talmud states that the Holy Altar "cries" when a couple divorces.[9] This statement helps us to see the greater picture: This is not just about me, my wants, and interests. It's about a bigger plan, about my role in this world.[10]

---

7. See Deuteronomy 22:13 and Rambam, *Hilchot Ishut* 1:2.

8. As with everything, the Torah is the guideline for when and how a divorce should be sought. See *Shulchan Aruch, Even HaEzer* 119:1.

9. Talmud, *Gittin* 90b.

10. Marital harmony is so important that G-d will even allow His Name to be erased to preserve it. Erasing G-d's Name is a serious biblical prohibition. But there is one exception to this. During the time of the Temple, if a woman was found alone with another man, casting doubts concerning her faithfulness, a procedure was followed to verify whether she had, indeed, been unfaithful. Her husband would bring her to the Temple, and there the *kohen* would prepare a parchment with G-d's Name on it. The parchment was then placed into water, erasing the Name, and the water was given to the woman to drink. If she had been unfaithful, she would immediately feel the consequences. (If the husband was ever unfaithful, this technique would have no effect on his wife.) Our

Elsewhere in the Torah, we find that when G-d reprimanded Avraham regarding his wife Sarah's doubting that she would be able to conceive a child, G-d said, "Why did she say that she is old?"

If you look at the text carefully, you will find that she actually said, "My master [i.e., husband] is old." Why did G-d change her words? Our Rabbis teach[11] that here we see the importance of marital harmony. To avoid a conflict between Avraham and his wife, G-d was willing to conceal the complete truth.

When a person takes this cosmic perspective into account, he will be more determined to make things work and not get caught up in small issues.

Think about it. It isn't logical that two people with different backgrounds and personalities can merge and find common ground. Confrontation and controversy are more likely. They have a greater chance of succeeding when they have a higher goal and mission to bind them so that they can use their individual and often opposite character traits for a common purpose. [12]

When we have a higher purpose and goal, we can manage our natural differences. As long as we can appreciate that our union is Divine and that the marriage is sacred, we overcome all odds and challenges, and ultimately, endure and succeed.

Rabbis explain that to preserve marital harmony, G-d is willing to forego His own honor (*Vayikra Rabbah* 9:9).

11. Talmud, *Yevamot* 65b.

12. There is a well-known Talmudic saying regarding marriage, "If a man and woman are meritorious, the Divine Presence will rest between them. If not, they will be consumed by fire" (*Sotah* 17a). This is based on the fact that the Hebrew words for "man" and "woman" are *ish* and *ishah*. Both contain the word for "fire," *eish*. In addition to *eish*, the Hebrew word for "man" also has the letter *yud*, while the Hebrew word for woman has the letter *hei*. Together, these two letters spell G-d's Name. As long as G-d is present in the relationship, there is harmony. If you remove G-d from the marriage, all that remains is the fire of strife.

Two people may love and care for each other, but without a Divine force, what is to bond temporal human beings eternally? Such a bond is necessary, for, besides being two strangers with different personalities and backgrounds, a man and a woman differ biologically, emotionally, and psychologically and will undergo many transitions in their lives.[13]

This works both ways. When we make the effort to maintain marital harmony, then we can merit to have G-d's Presence among us. And if G-d is an integral part of our lives, it will be easier to achieve marital harmony.[14]

Why did G-d set things up this way? Why is it so important for two opposites to live together and maintain a relationship?

In fact, why did G-d create us this way in the first place? Men could have been created so that they would be naturally spiritual and would never act selfishly.

But G-d didn't create us that way. Instead, we were created with a strong animal nature. We naturally seek to fulfill our desires and pleasures. As a counterbalance, however, He also gave us a holy and G-dly soul that aspires to do what's right.

It is up to us to transform our physical, instinctive nature into a higher level of awareness and behavior.

This is one of the purposes of Judaism: to train ourselves to curtail these passions. This is why we have commandments that

---

13. Jacobson, *Toward a Meaningful Life*, p. 50.

14. We pray in the Amidah every day, "*Oseh shalom bimromav Hu ya'aseh shalom aleinu...* — He makes peace on High; He shall bestow peace upon us..." The Midrash explains (*Devarim Rabbah* 5:2) that this refers to G-d Who makes peace between the angels Michael and Gavriel. What is the conflict between these angels and how does G-d make peace between them? Michael is the angel of kindness; Gavriel is the angel of discipline. Since they are opposites, they don't see eye to eye. However, they both realize that they report to a Higher Authority, G-d Himself. In this way, G-d makes peace between these opposite forces.

pertain to all aspects of our physical lives — our eating habits, work ethics, family values, finances... and marriage. All these laws help us transform our selfish desires into selfless acts. For example, the need to earn a livelihood and accumulate wealth is a natural part of living in this world. By giving charity and being honest in our business dealings, we elevate this physical need to a Divine service. As the Chassidic saying goes, "Making the animal into a human is the greatest miracle."

This is the whole purpose of our existence: to subdue our animal nature and develop our spiritual nature — and thereby fulfill G-d's plan in Creation to make an abode for Him in this lowly world through the spiritual efforts of the human being.[15] If G-d had created us solely with a spiritual nature, we wouldn't be in this world in the first place.

The question that we have to ask ourselves is, Is this the way that we perceive our lives? Are we trying to be better people and improve the world we live in? Or are we looking primarily for the personal satisfaction that we tend to associate with success, wealth, status, and pleasure?

Especially today, the pursuit of pleasure has become man's primary goal. This is not the product of a conscious decision, but rather it's instinctive. However, Judaism affirms that although this is our natural state, we can overcome our impulses.

This is the difference between the human and the animal. Though an animal can be trained to exhibit certain behaviors, it is incapable of changing its nature by cognitive means. It doesn't have the ability to think and make choices about how to act. A human being, on the other hand, can change his conduct by making rational decisions. So while you have humans who have

---

15. *Tanya*, ch. 36.

chosen to become vegetarians, we have yet to see a tiger making such a choice. Animals are programmed; we aren't.

All this supports our original premise: Men are naturally bound to pursue the three P's of Prestige, Power, and Pleasure, while women seek the three A's — Achievement, Appearance, and Affection, things that are related to their need for self-esteem rather than any ego trip. But in addition to the animal drive, we have a Divine spark within us. It is the consciousness, the inner voice, that encourages us to live by absolute values based on the Torah. When we listen to our inner awareness, we are able to shun our animal inclination and let the G-dly part of us lead the way to perfection and true happiness.

This is what it means to keep G-d in your marriage. If you focus on the mission — to be dedicated to your spouse rather than pursuing only your own pleasures — you will be pleasantly surprised at how much better your relationship will become on all levels.[16]

Knowing that your spouse's behavior is rooted in the three A's or the three P's will help you form realistic expectations of your spouse and handle difficult situations in a constructive way. When you bring G-d into your marriage, your chances of making it last improve dramatically.

---

16. It's interesting to note that the Aramaic translation for "love" is *hav*, which means "give." The more you give, the more you get.

11 Make It Work, Make the Effort

WE ESTABLISHED THAT CHANGING the way we view our spouse and our approach to marriage will go a long way to changing many marital issues. It will pave the way toward a more fulfilling marriage, to the road that leads to true happiness. But changing our mindset is only the first step.

I Want to Be Your Friend — Let's Get Divorced

IN WESTERN COUNTRIES, OVER half of all marriages end up in divorce. This statistic is very alarming. But what I find of even greater concern is that many of these divorced couples remain good friends. They go out for dinner once in a while. They can have coffee together and normal conversations. If you ask them, "Why did you get divorced?" they'll answer, "We weren't compatible."

But this is hard to comprehend — if they are able to be friends, they must have been compatible. It's more likely that one or both weren't giving the other what they wanted or needed, and rather than working it out, divorce was the easier option.

People have asked me on many occasions, "Should couples stay married if they are unhappy?"

There isn't any clear-cut answer to that question. There are situations when a divorce is necessary and, for that very reason, the Torah discusses divorce as an option. But it is the emergency exit, not even the back door. It should be used only if the relationship becomes intolerable, and staying married is more damaging to everyone involved (including the children) than ending the marriage. But if a divorced couple is on friendly terms, their divorce was probably avoidable.

A farmer in the former Soviet Union was asked if he would give the Communist Party ten acres of land. "Of course I would." "How about a thousand cows?" "Certainly." "Five hundred goats?" "Definitely." "Two hundred sheep?" "This, too, with pleasure." "Twelve chickens?" "No way." "If you are willing to give so much more, why aren't you willing to give twelve chickens?" "Because I actually own twelve chickens."

By no means am I suggesting that divorced couples need to maintain a state of war after the marriage has dissolved. There needs to be a cordial relationship where they can get along together for the good of the children. But there is a long way between a cordial relationship that does not put the kids in the middle of your affairs and a friendly relationship that prompts you to go out for coffee on Tuesdays.

What's behind this trend toward short-term marriages and long-term friendships?

In many cases, the couple was committed only to a relationship that made them feel good. They weren't prepared for the sacrifice and effort such a commitment requires. As a result, they felt they could get divorced as soon as one partner realized that "my needs are not being met" and "my expectations have not been realized." In essence, the party initiating the divorce stopped saying, "I love you," and began to say, "I really love me."

Given this all-too-common situation, I think that the question isn't, "Why are so many people getting divorced?" but, "Why aren't there *more* divorces?"

> A young unmarried woman was discussing with the Lubavitcher Rebbe some prospective matches that had been suggested to her, and she explained why none of them appealed to her. The Rebbe smiled. "You have read too many romance novels," he replied. "Love is not the overwhelming, blinding emotions we find in the world of fiction. Real love is an emotion that intensifies throughout life. It is the small, everyday acts of being together that make love flourish. It is sharing and caring and respecting one another. It is building a life together, a family and a home. As two lives unite to form one, over time there is a point where each partner feels a part of the other, where each partner can no longer visualize life without the other at his or her side."[1]

Marriage can thrive on one condition: if both spouses are willing to work on it together. You need to be proactive. Turn off the cruise control and take charge of your relationship.

Take Charge of Your Relationship

LET'S SEE HOW THIS relates to the three P's and the three A's.

Male self-esteem depends primarily on the three P's — Prestige, Power, and Pleasure. As we discussed in Chapter 5, this basically suggests that a husband's self-esteem does not depend primarily on his wife. It suggests that as long as he has health,

---

1. Jacobson, *Toward a Meaningful Life*, p. 57.

status, success, and a normal standard of living, he will feel ful-filled, and he will then be able to focus on making his wife happy and content.

For the wife, her self-esteem depends on the three A's of Affection, Achievement, and Appearance. Affection, which de-rives from feeling loved, cherished, and cared for is clearly the strongest element in the equation. For a woman to direct her energy to her husband, she needs him to build her self-esteem. It seems that only after a husband does his part can he expect his wife to be able to focus on giving him what he needs.

Based on this, we can deduce that the harmony in the home is the husband's responsibility. Why? Because while he is not de-pendent primarily on his wife for his self-worth, he has a strong influence on his wife's feelings of self-worth. If a man treats his wife with dignity, respect, love and kindness, giving her the at-tention, affection, and appreciation that she desires, she will be happy. If he neglects her emotional needs and focuses on his personal life and interests, she will be miserable.

We find this idea in the Torah. It is written, "A person who has built a home, planted a vineyard, or consecrated a woman, but has not inaugurated his home, harvested his vineyard, or married his bride, is exempt from the army."[2] The Torah con-cludes, "*V'simach et ishto asher lakach* — He must bring joy to the wife he has acquired." Note that the three exemptions could cor-respond to the three P's: Prestige, Power, and Pleasure. The home corresponds to Prestige, the vineyard to Power, and the wife to Pleasure. The Torah's admonition not to "forget to bring joy to your wife" is telling the husband, "Don't forget to provide for her needs so she will be satisfied and happy."

This is the opposite of what most people have accepted as the

---

2. Deuteronomy 24:5.

formula for a successful marriage. Many people think that the success of a marriage depends primarily on the wife. It depends on how she treats her husband, on her demeanor, on her always being attentive to his needs and wants. If she is always in good spirits and is always available to be her husband's support and tolerate his ego trip and selfishness, everything will be fine.

However, marriage depends on *both* partners doing their part. It's not realistic to expect a wife to sacrifice herself without receiving in return; it's necessary for both sides to fulfill their commitment and responsibilities. But it's more natural for a woman to be a caring and giving spouse. A man must put in more effort and dedication to provide his wife with the affection and attention she needs, since this is not his nature.

> The truth is that the happiest couples relate as equals, with her treating him like a king and him treating her like a queen. Men are less spontaneously nurturing than women. By nature, a woman expresses her love more freely and derives her deepest satisfaction by devoting herself to the man she loves (*Berachot* 30b). Taking care of others does not come as spontaneously or naturally to men as it does to women. Little girls spend a lot of their play time in nurturing activities, something little boys do rarely.[3]

If the husband does his part in providing emotional support, the wife will usually fulfill hers. But often, even if a woman fulfills her responsibilities as a dedicated wife, this is far from an assurance that her husband will do his share of providing the affection she desires.

> According to Kabbalah, an important principle of creation is that the male is the giver and the female is the receiver. The

---

3. Adahan, *It's All a Gift*, p. 104.

husband resembles the sun, and the wife resembles the moon. ... the light that he shines on her. Therefore, her darkness is a sign of his insufficient illumination.[4]

We learn this idea from the commandment of circumcision. The Midrash states[5] that the evil Roman emperor Turnus Rufus asked Rabbi Akiva, "Why do you circumcise your children? If G-d wanted the male to be circumcised, He could have created him already circumcised."

Rabbi Akiva replied, "The reason G-d wanted us to circumcise males is for men to participate in perfecting the world. Therefore, He created man imperfect and required him to complete the Creation. This applies not only to this one area of the body, but to all areas of life."

Men were created imperfect — they need to be reminded that there is work to do. But women were created without the same level of imperfection. That is why, regarding women, the Talmud states, "A woman is already considered circumcised from birth."[6] She doesn't need to do anything to confirm the circumcision covenant between G-d and Avraham. The covenant is "inscribed" in her nature, not her flesh. For this reason, there is no mitzvah of circumcision for women. There is no reason for them to wear a kipa, tzitzit, or tefillin — all physical reminders to help the male rein in his ego.[7]

Women have a greater natural orientation toward spirituality than men, which is why the Sages say that the reward promised

---

4. Arush, *The Garden of Peace*, p. 49.

5. *Midrash Tanchuma, Tazria* 5.

6. *Avodah Zarah* 27a.

7. This does not mean that women don't have obligations. They are still required to observe the prohibitions and certain positive commandments. But they have fewer obligations because they have less to perfect.

to women in the World to Come is greater than that promised to men (*Berachot* 17a). This is why women, unlike their husbands, did not succumb to the temptation of worshipping the golden calf (Tur, *Orach Chaim* 417). And the Torah was given first to women and only afterwards to men because they are more zealous in performing mitzvot (*Shemot Rabbah* 28:2).[8]

A similar view is presented by [Rabbi] Samson Raphael Hirsch who suggests that women are endowed with superior motivation and inspiration to serve G-d. "G-d's Torah takes it for granted that our women have greater fervor and more faithful enthusiasm for their G-d-serving calling."[9]

If you apply the concept of covenant (i.e., bond) to marriage, it fits quite nicely. In essence, the covenant calls for men to control and curtail their egos. It requires of them to sacrifice a part of themselves for G-d. This reminds them that they are imperfect and need to improve themselves and hence the world by becoming givers to others and to G-d. Women are beyond that stage. They are inherently better at caring and giving, which is what G-d really wants from all of mankind, Jew and non-Jew alike.

To illustrate this point with another law:

According to Judaism, the commandment to "be fruitful and multiply"[10] applies only to men. Women have no biblical obligation to procreate. On the surface, this law seems irrational. Without women, mankind could not reproduce. Why would G-d give them an exemption?

The Lubavitcher Rebbe, *zy"a*, explains:[11] If men weren't "commanded" by G-d to have children, many of them would choose to

---

8. Feldman, *The River, the Kettle, and the Bird*, p. 55.

9. Rabbi Raphael Aron, *Spirituality and Intimacy* (Devora Publishing, 2008), p. 49.

10. Genesis 1:28.

11. *Sefer Hasichot* 5751, p. 86.

live a more selfish life. Why worry about children? Let me enjoy life! But a woman by nature wants to have a family and offspring. For this reason, it wasn't necessary to obligate her to procreate.

Also, a man is responsible for providing three things to his wife: food, clothing (shelter), and marital relations.[12] Yet nowhere in the Torah are women *commanded* to provide anything for their husbands! The Torah understands that men can easily forget that here is another human being who also has needs; it doesn't want men to neglect their wives for any reason. So the Torah tells them, "Remember your wife. Make sure she is your priority when you fulfill this commandment." The Torah doesn't command a similar responsibility to women. Why? She naturally thinks about her spouse's needs.

Bottom line: Man has to rein in his ego (remember: he's the one who naturally pursues Power and Prestige) in order to make sure he fulfills his responsibilities to procreate and to make his wife happy.

How does the idea that men need to take more responsibility for marital harmony reconcile with the idea that "*chochmat nashim bantah beitah* — the wisdom of women builds her home"?[13] This saying suggests that the success of marriage depends on the woman.

This does not contradict our premise. Since men are more selfish by nature, a woman must be able to navigate different situations in the marriage while enabling her husband to believe that his power is intact and has not been compromised.

Women are usually more accommodating and focused on the family; they are usually willing to make the effort to avoid

---

12. See Rambam, *Hilchot Ishut* 12:1.
13. Proverbs 14:1.

confrontations and maintain the peace in the home.[14] In that sense, "it is the wisdom of women that builds her home." But for a truly fulfilling marriage, the husband needs to make a great effort to be attentive and giving; it should not all be up to the woman.

> The Mishnah states, "The disciples of our father Avraham possess a generous eye, a humble spirit, and a modest soul. The disciples of the wicked Bilaam possess an evil eye, an arrogant spirit, and a gluttonous soul" (*Avot* 5:19). Rabbi Ovadiah of Bartenura comments that the three character traits of Bilaam represent three ideas. The "evil eye" is found in an envious person who is unhappy to see anyone more successful than him. An arrogant spirit can be understood by its literal meaning. A gluttonous soul refers to the individual who desires physical pleasures.
>
> These three traits have a striking parallel to the three P's: Prestige, Power, and Pleasure. The message of the Mishnah is that we should strive to be among the students of Avraham and not among the students of Bilaam. Despite a man's instinctive need to pursue Prestige, Pleasure, and Power, his mission is to subjugate those needs in order to acquire "a generous eye, a humble spirit, and a modest soul." Similarly, the Mishnah also says, "Envy, lust, and honor remove a person from the world" (*Avot* 4:21). The message is the same: The pursuits of prestige, honor, envy, power, lust, and pleasure need to be curtailed in favor of higher pursuits.

---

14. The wife of On ben Peles, for example, ensured that her husband did not join Korach's rebellion. If he had, he would have died along with the rest of Korach's followers. See Talmud, *Sanhedrin* 110a.

Love = Effort

IT IS NOT EASY to do something that is against your nature. It's hard for a man to expend so much effort to fulfill his wife's needs when they seem so trivial. Isn't it enough that he provides for her and loves her? Why does he have to constantly shower attention on her to prove his love? But that is precisely why marriage is such hard work. It requires us to do things that are not instinctive, that demand not only discipline but awareness of another's needs that are so different from ours. For women, this is easier to envision, but for men it is much more difficult.

This brings to mind a common expression: "I am a Jew at heart. The fact that I love G-d is enough. I don't need to do anything to show it." Imagine a husband who tells his wife that he loves her once in a while and expects that this should be enough for her. What type of love is this? If one is not willing to sacrifice, this is by no means love.[15]

If we truly love someone, we are willing to make an effort for that person. The same applies to our relationship with G-d. Our love for Him should be expressed by our willingness to do things that we might not like. This is one of the reasons that in Judaism we have a number of commandments that are super-rational — *chukim* (statutes). There are no reasons given for these commandments. We do them because G-d told us to. Couldn't G-d explain all the laws instead of commanding us to fulfill some that we can't comprehend?

This is precisely the point. If we understood the reason for everything we do, this would not be considered an absolute relationship; it would be a convenient one. How would a marriage function when one spouse tells the other, "I will do only the things I feel like doing?" Can such a relationship last?

---

15. See Chapter 8, "Love Is Not an Accident."

It Takes Real Confidence

THE IDEA OF FOCUSING on your spouse's needs more than on your own can be frightening. This approach appears detrimental to your own self-esteem. It seems that focusing on your spouse's needs means you must ignore your own needs and desires. Although this approach might be beneficial for the marriage, won't it be detrimental to your personal fulfillment? What about taking care of your own needs?

A person without self-esteem doesn't live; he exists. In fact, it's impossible to be a centered and balanced human being without basic self-esteem.

How can we reconcile this?

These approaches are *not* mutually exclusive; they are complementary. Only a person with healthy self-esteem is able to focus on another person's needs and wishes. Someone who suffers from low self-esteem will find this extremely difficult. Why is that?

We all need to perceive that we have value; this is crucial for our mental and emotional well-being. Furthermore, self-esteem is the barometer with which we measure our value. A person who doubts his worth — who suffers from a deficient self-esteem — requires others to constantly fill this void. How can this person fulfill his spouse's needs when he is so dependent on his spouse to lift his own self-esteem?

Renowned lecturer and marriage authority Rabbi Manis Friedman says that marriages typically occur when both parties are adults (rather than teens). Only when one is mature enough to understand what another person requires can one be a good spouse.

> This is what distinguishes us from the children we once were. Having gotten bigger than our own egos, we can now take someone else's ego seriously. The next step, the logical step, the G-dly step, is to appreciate someone else, to respect someone else, to make someone else feel secure, and for this we are now qualified.

That's why we wait to be married until we are ready to be married, when we are grown and able to take on the responsibility for another person's mortal soul — having finally mastered our own.

Then we remind ourselves, "The needs of my mortal soul are there so I can understand what another person is feeling and take care of that person's needs; to take care of my own would be hedonistic. Now that I have felt the need for respect, for appreciation, and for security, I know how to respect, appreciate, and make someone else feel secure."[16]

I would approach this idea from a slightly different angle. Only when I have developed a solid self-esteem do I have the strength and ability to dedicate myself to my spouse. Only an individual who has a healthy self-esteem will be able to focus on fulfilling a spouse's needs and wants. Therefore, part of my self-esteem should be based on how good a spouse I am, on how much I am *giving*, instead of how much I am getting from the marriage.

By building my self-esteem on the basis of giving, I will be strong enough to give to my spouse without feeling threatened that my needs won't be met.

For a woman, this may not be enough. Unlike her husband, she needs affection and fulfillment for her self-esteem. She may therefore need to look for external ways to seek fulfillment, just as her husband has external ways to build his self-esteem. In this way, she will be less dependent on her husband for her self-worth. By building her self-esteem in other ways, she will be less affected when she feels she is not getting the attention she wants.

Marriage is hard work. It requires doing the opposite of what is instinctive in order to provide what our spouses need. For a man, this means doing things for his wife even if they don't make

---

16. Friedman, *Doesn't Anyone Blush Anymore?* (2012), p. 23.

sense to him. For a woman, it may mean accepting that she will not always feel that she is her husband's top priority, that she will not always be the center of his attention, and trying not to interpret all of his actions as signs that he doesn't love her.

Either way, it is a great effort. But an effort that is well worth it, one that will lead to a more fulfilling, happier marriage where everyone gets what they need.

It's not enough to change your perspective about your spouse; you have to be proactive: Focus on what you can do for your spouse rather than on what you can get (or what you are not getting). To truly give, however, you need to overcome your nature and have strong self-esteem.

12 Let's Get Practical: How to Please Your Spouse

"**A** WIFE SHOULD TREAT HER husband like a king. A husband should love his wife more than he loves himself."[1] With these few words, the Rambam (Maimonides) presents the complete formula for a successful marriage. Here, too, we see evidence of the three P's and the three A's. Men require an ego boost (Prestige and Power): "You are my king!" Women, on the other hand, need to be loved (Affection).

What do men need to do for their wives so they feel loved? The answer is so obvious that it may come as a surprise. Men have to show their wives that they are indeed their priority, ranking way above work, clients, friends, and hobbies. Whenever a wife doubts her place on her husband's list of priorities, she becomes anxious. But a husband who keeps his wife at (or near) the top of his priority list will have a very happy wife with healthy self-esteem.

The story is told about the time the Lubavitcher Rebbe, *zy"a*,

---

1. Rambam, *Hilchot Ishut*, ch. 15.

and his wife, the Rebbetzin, lived in Paris, years before he assumed leadership of the movement. It was a Shabbat afternoon, and they were taking a stroll.

A certain individual approached the Rebbe and said, "I don't feel it's appropriate for a Jew of your stature to be taking a stroll on Shabbat afternoon."

He was implying that the Rebbe should be spending his time learning Torah instead.

The Rebbe's response was direct. "When the king's daughter wants to go for a walk, one must accompany her."

There are times when I would prefer to be studying. But if my wife wants to get out of the house and would like me to join her, that becomes my priority.

Over fifteen hundred years ago the Talmudic Sage Rabbi Yosi declared, "I have never called my spouse 'my wife' but 'my home.'"[2] He wanted us to know that his wife was more than a servant or even a manager. She was the chief operating officer (COO) of his household. Although Rabbi Yosi probably didn't think in terms of the three A's, he knew how important it is to appreciate his wife's accomplishments. The woman has the great task of raising a family, and hence deserves respect and displays of appreciation for the high level of achievement she continually attains.

> They say that women want their husbands to change, but it never happens. Men want their wives to stay the same, but that never happens, either.

Marital bliss and success rotate around one central axis — a wife's knowledge that she holds first place in her husband's list of

---

2. Talmud, *Shabbat* 118b.

priorities. She wants to be the most important part of his life. He should strive to make her feel that way.

A husband should seize every opportunity to show her that she holds first place. He should remind her constantly that she is his top priority and his actions should bear witness to his words all the time. When she needs something, he should jump to do it. When she opens her mouth, he should lend an ear as if she is about to say the most important thing in the world.

> When a wife sees that a husband does everything in his power to please her, then she'll really feel like she's in first place in his life. This feeling gives her indescribable joy, strength, and vitality. He is ultimately the one that benefits from all his sacrifices for her. Her payback is tenfold from whatever he invests in making her feel like she is number one.[3]

7

Make Time for Your Spouse

ON A TRIP TO Israel, I met the *rosh yeshivah* of the Tzemach Tzeddek *kollel* (where married men study). During a car ride to Jerusalem, he shared this story.

Shortly after his marriage, he was in New York and received a private audience with the Lubavitcher Rebbe, *zy"a*.[4]

Prior to the meeting, he wrote down his daily schedule. It began quite early in the morning and ended very late at night. Every part of his day was packed with studying or teaching. He was convinced that this was a pretty impressive work schedule and that the Rebbe would be pleased. The Rebbe's reaction was totally unexpected.

---

3. Arush, *The Garden of Peace*, p. 63.

4. Rabbi Menachem Mendel Schneerson (1902–1994), seventh Rebbe of Chabad Lubavitch dynasty. Established centers worldwide to preserve Judaism and reach out to Jews in remote places of the world.

"What time do you go home?" the Rebbe inquired.

"I get home very late at night," the *rosh yeshivah* said.

"You can't find a little time during the day to go home? Not even ten minutes? This is inconceivable! You're married! It's not fair that your wife should be alone from so early in the morning until so late at night."

This is an eye-opening story for young married men who are full-time Torah scholars. Studying Torah is indeed a fundamental and great mitzvah. They must, however, realize that even when men are doing something of great value, they still need to be in tune with the needs of their spouse.

A couple once appeared before a therapist and poured out their woes and troubles. The expert listened politely and at the end stated, "It's just stress. If you can lower your stress levels you will be fine. I suggest that you go out once a week. This will surely help you."

Several weeks later, they visited the therapist. "How is it going?" he asked.

"Great," the husband replied. "We followed your advice and it worked perfectly."

"I am pleased to hear how well you are doing," the therapist responded. "Can you share details about your experience?"

"Certainly. I go out on Tuesdays and she goes out on Wednesdays."

Another area where a husband can be in tune with his wife is shopping. Most women enjoy shopping more than men. For them, the mall is like an amusement park. Even just window-shopping is fun. Men, by contrast, usually don't feel fulfilled by looking at merchandise they have no interest in buying, to say the least. It makes no sense to go to the mall with no purpose other than to walk around. (They would, however, prefer that their wives liked to window-shop more and purchase less!)

If going to the mall is an activity that your wife enjoys, accompany her. When she sees that you truly care for her, and that you'd even go shopping to make her happy, she may be willing to join you for an outing that would not be her first choice.

> A man once stood before a judge and stated, "Your honor, I can't pay my bills."
>
> "Why not?" asked the judge.
>
> "All the money that my wife saves on sales is leading me into bankruptcy."

The husband, on the other hand, wants a wife who will greet him warmly when he arrives home. If she is on the telephone, she should politely tell her friend (or mother or sister) that she has to hang up now.

The time when your husband comes home is not the time to update your Twitter account or catch up on e-mails. Close the laptop and give your husband your full attention. He also appreciates it when dinner is ready when he gets home and likes to have his wife's company when he sits down to eat, even if she ate earlier with the children.

Whether at the mall or the dinner table, the more activities you share, the easier it is to solidify your relationship. Spending time together is the main opportunity to show your spouse that he or she is a priority in your life.

Give Him Space

WOMEN NEED AFFECTION AND attention for their self-esteem, so they appreciate when their husbands spend time with them. But there is another side to that coin. People (i.e., husbands) need their space. The delicate challenge is how to balance one's wants with those of one's partner.

I was once visited by an angry wife. Her husband would often travel for business and now he was planning a trip alone to a family event in another country. His wife wanted him to go for only two days and return to be with her or to cancel the trip altogether.

I tried to calm her down and make her see that she wasn't being entirely rational. Her husband should be able to attend a family gathering and even stay a few additional days.

"I know that this is not easy for you," I told her. "You don't particularly care for his family, and you also suffer from the fact that your husband needs to travel so often for business. That's what's keeping you from accepting the idea that taking this family trip is the proper thing to do."

Later, after she calmed down, she realized that she was feeling jealous because she wanted to spend more time with her husband. Usually, she would be within her rights to ask him to spend some time with her, especially since he was so often away from home. But in this case, traveling to see his family was the right thing to do.

It Doesn't Have to Be a Sacrifice

ALTHOUGH IT IS NOW clear that we must be willing to sacrifice some of our desires in order to please our spouse, it's more practical to see how we can use our P's and A's to unite us.

Sometimes I wonder why G-d created us with the need to eat. He could have created us differently. If a bear can hibernate for the winter, why didn't He just make us the same way? I am sure many people would be very happy if they didn't have to worry about eating for a few months out of the year.

Practically speaking, a huge amount of the world's economy depends on the food industry. On a spiritual plane, eating can bring us tremendous merit — many of the mitzvot are related to food. But our need to eat brings us an additional benefit.

Food plays an essential role in keeping the family unit together. Every person in the family has a full schedule of activities. If we didn't need to eat, we could probably go without seeing each other for weeks. So G-d created a need that we also enjoy. It's called food. Since food brings us to the table at dinnertime, it gives us the opportunity to talk and connect with our family.

The same applies to marriage. Couples need to make an effort to spend time together in order to strengthen and nurture their connection to each other. This is especially important to the woman, who translates the time spent with her husband as an emotional connection with him, as a sense of feeling loved, which is so essential to her. For the man, spending time with his wife helps him stay in tune with her needs.

This does not mean that you have to do something you don't enjoy just to make your spouse happy. Ideally, it's good to find activities that you both like to do and do them together — long walks, a sport, studying together, eating out, visiting museums or other interesting places, even cooking together.

Or, how about board games? As the family grows, this activity can include the kids. There are the all-time classics like Risk, Monopoly, Chinese Checkers, and Clue, but there are also a lot of other types of games — word games, strategy games, adventure games — that the whole family can enjoy.

Why not find a project you can do as a team? Bake for a special occasion, paint a room, or clean out the attic. Better yet, find a charitable cause in which you can both participate. For the more intellectual couple, reading and talking about current events can be quite productive and meaningful. Some couples enjoy discussing Torah-related subjects, inspirational stories of holy Jews, and new insights into the weekly Torah portion. Of course, the children and their accomplishments at home and in school, and their achievements in sports or other extracurricular activities, are topics of interest to both partners.

In 1978, the Lubavitcher Rebbe, *zy'a*, suffered a heart attack and, after several weeks, miraculously recovered. His doctors realized that the Rebbe would need to change his schedule. He had been spending most of his time in Torah study and attending to the hundreds of daily letters, requests, and petitions from people across the globe. The medical team felt that his system would no longer tolerate the fast pace. But to suggest major lifestyle changes to a towering personality was no small feat. Wisely, the doctors chose a tactic that was respectful and reverent.

"Rebbe," they asked, "what part of your schedule is non-negotiable?"

To everyone's surprise, he said, "The time I spend having tea with my wife."

In order to develop this attitude, you need to see your spouse as a friend, not just as a husband or wife. Friends enjoy spending time together. This feeling is exactly what every couple needs in order to achieve a lasting relationship. Naturally, a physical and emotional connection can keep the couple united during the early and middle years of a marriage, but for a long-term marriage, the friendship part is essential.

A woman once told me that during their courtship, she would accompany her fiancé to watch Sunday football, although she really didn't care for sports. Obviously this was not an activity that would keep them together long after their wedding. They would have to find something that both enjoyed doing and that they could do together.

Some couples work together at the same company or run a business together. For those who can successfully team up with their spouses at work, this is unique and beneficial. But if they disagree at work and are not able to work things out harmoniously, this will be detrimental to their relationship.

The more activities you share, the easier it will be to solidify your relationship. Spending time together is an opportunity to show your spouse that he or she is a priority in your life.

Maintaining a Balance

YEARS AGO, I TOOK a time-management course. The presenter asked participants to write down everything on our daily "to do" list. Then we had to rate each activity according to its priority. The number one meant that the activity was very important, two meant that the activity was somewhat important, and three meant that the activity was the least important. We found that level-three activities occupied most of our days, even though they were the least critical.

Spending time with your family is most likely in the level one category and checking e-mails a level three, but the reality is that we get caught up with the threes and we don't get around to the ones. Unless we block out time for what we consider to be truly a priority, we'll never get to it. Deep down, marriage is the priority of every spouse. But this priority is often overwhelmed by day-to-day responsibilities and tasks. As a result, it's put on the back burner and at times becomes completely forgotten.

> A manager told his employee, "Jack, I need you to do this assignment."
>
> Jack answered back, "Sorry, boss, I'm overloaded with work."
>
> "Do it during your lunch hour," the manager suggested.
>
> "I am already working during my lunch break."
>
> Jack's manager had the final say. "Take a longer lunch hour if you need to — just make sure the work gets done!"

If your spouse is one of your priorities, make sure that she is on your schedule. All it takes is a phone call or a text message to let her know you are thinking about her.

Some homes operate under an unwritten agreement: I work. You take care of the household. I don't talk to you about work. You don't talk to me about the home. This approach is not healthy for marriage. It basically says, "I will live my life as I see fit and you live yours." This does not bring people together, it drives them apart.

The Mishnah teaches that, according to one opinon, this is the way of Sodom, the most wicked city mentioned in the Torah. "One who says, 'What is mine is mine and what is yours is yours' [has chosen] the middle path. Others suggest that this is the way of Sodom."[5] Instead, we should take the next path that the Mishnah describes, "The one who says, 'What is mine is yours and what is yours is yours' — this is a *chassid* (pious Jew)."

There was a time when women were so busy working and caring for the family, that there was little time left for them to think about whether they were feeling fulfilled. Today most people are blessed with easier lives, and making time to spend with their spouses has become a greater issue. It's extremely important to make time for analyzing the relationships in our lives, and most importantly our marriage, and to ensure that both parties are happy and satisfied.

Shower Your Spouse with Compliments

A husband needs to be constantly on the lookout for opportunities to lavish compliments and kind words on his wife. Her good looks, her cooking, her ideas, her hard work, how well she deals with the children, and her housekeeping all deserve praise on a regular basis. Telling her how good she looks in what she's wearing will always give her joy. The more that a husband finds to praise and compliment his wife about, the happier she will be.[6]

---

5. *Avot* 1:10.
6. Arush, *The Garden of Peace*, p. 111.

Some people find the whole idea of giving compliments strange. We expect people to do certain tasks, and we don't typically compliment them for "doing their job." If the bus driver took my kid to school, does he deserve a compliment? Common courtesy suggests that it's enough to say "Thank you," but we don't need to lavish words of praise on him. How about the bank teller who processes our deposit or the gas-station attendant who fills our tank with gas? These people are simply doing their jobs. If one day they do their jobs in an exceptional manner — the bus driver waits when your child is late, or the teller works quickly, or the gas-station attendant washes your car windows — then they deserve to be paid a compliment. Otherwise a "thank you" should suffice.

In marriage, too, there are certain expectations. There are certain "jobs" that each spouse contributes. When a spouse performs those tasks, usually there is no verbal recognition besides a curt, "Thanks." More often, the efforts of one's spouse go unnoticed or at least unmentioned. But many times, especially at the end of a difficult day, your spouse can probably use words of comfort and encouragement. The woman especially, who seeks Affection, needs this. Unfortunately, this positive reinforcement seldom comes. We get used to producing without receiving much feedback.

And what happens when we don't get around to completing our daily activities, either because we are overworked, stressed-out, or have just overlooked a part of the routine? Chances are we will hear about it, sometimes politely and sometimes with disappointment and even complaint.

So what ends up occurring? The husband and wife spend 80 percent of their time complaining! You can be sure that this is detrimental to a relationship.

> A family was getting ready to go on a field trip. The wife said to her husband, "How about if today you get the kids ready while I honk the horn?"

When this imbalance is pointed out either indirectly or directly, the reaction is usually, "Of course I value all that you do and the effort and sacrifices you make." But how should your spouse know your feelings of appreciation unless you communicate them?

For a marriage to thrive, most of the communication should be not complaints or accusations, but *compliments* and *praises*. Keep displeasure or criticism down to a minimum of your communication.

Once, I attended an event and began chatting with one of the members of the community. He told me he was a lucky man because his wife was very thrifty. At that moment his wife appeared. I took the opportunity to relate her husband's praise.

"He should compliment me to my face," she said, "and not take me for granted and just criticize me when things go wrong."

"This is what I've come to expect from you," he retorted.

It was clear to me that she was being sincere, so after she left, I said, "Pardon me, but it's important to tell your wife how special and important she is to you. It is the smart way to live. Just because men don't have the same need for praise doesn't mean their wives should have to do without."

When we don't make it a point to notice our spouse's efforts and accomplishments, we have stopped seeing them as independent beings. This is unhealthy in a marriage.

> We have previously noted that common courtesy calls for expressing gratitude for favors received. But showing simple gratitude is not enough. It is necessary to shower her with praise for this. Because a wife needs to feel that she is beloved, her husband should leave her no room for doubt. Compliments and praise are the elemental way of creating this consciousness.[7]

---

7. Feldman, *The River, the Kettle and the Bird*, p. 49.

For as long as I can remember, my father would always compliment my mother after the Shabbat night meal and thank her for her effort and preparations. Each time, he did this with enthusiasm, as if it was the first and best meal he had ever received. And my mother appreciated the compliments every time, although she had heard them many times before.

Men also don't enjoy being taken for granted and need recognition, but they prefer that their spouses point out their achievements and ingenuity; they want to feel respected and competent. "I know I can always count on you."

"You make me feel secure and safe."

"You are a good example for the children."

"Your idea was very helpful and practical."

"I appreciate that you are a hard worker and so dedicated."

One of my memories of the Lubavitcher Rebbe, *zy"a*, is of how he made it a practice to acknowledge all the people who would assist him. Although holy and far removed from the mundane, the Rebbe would always remember to thank a person who did something for him. The individual who filled his cup for Kiddush received a nod as a means of thanks. The administrative secretary who would chauffeur him around was recognized for his service.

In addition, the Rebbe would be sure to make eye contact with every person who came to him, either to receive a dollar to give to charity or to receive wine from the cup on which he had recited *Birkat HaMazon* (Grace after Meals). Even at an advanced age, the Rebbe made this effort. I wondered why the Rebbe paused to look everyone in the eye when he could have saved plenty of time by focusing on the person's hand or cup. I came across an article that answered my question.

The article related the story of a boy who once went up to a famous sports figure to get an autograph. After waiting in line for a long time, he got it, but he felt crushed — the player didn't even look at him once. Looking a person in the eye communicates, "You are important to me. You are not a nuisance."

Make sure when expressing compliments that you maintain eye contact. This will show your spouse that you are sincere and truly appreciate them for who they are, and not just what they do. I firmly believe that a wife who feels that she is truly her husband's priority and is cherished and loved will naturally respond by making her husband feel like a king.

Make time for your spouse and compliment them.
Women, especially, like to be complimented,
while men need to know that they have their wife's respect.

13 Maintaining the Magic

REMEMBER WHAT YOUR RELATIONSHIP was like when you were engaged? Your spouse could do no wrong. Everything was perfect. No one could be better looking, nicer, or more interesting than the person you decided to marry. Certainly you never argued. If you did, you made up quickly and the argument was soon forgotten.

Do you still feel that way about your spouse? Is your spouse the same perfect human being that he or she was when you were dating?

Chances are, you no longer look at your spouse with the same rose-colored glasses. Things — little and big — annoy you. And you fight. What changed?

The Big Picture

I'M SURE YOU KNOW people who are good-looking, yet you've learned that they don't see themselves this way. If you know the person well, you might hear him make jokes about his big nose or speak disparagingly about his elephant ears. In fact, he may not even think he's good-looking at all. Why is it that you see such different things?

134

When you look at a person, you focus on the entire picture, and therefore your conclusion is (usually) positive. When the person looks at himself, he focuses on what he doesn't like. He zooms in on the little things that bother him and overlooks the whole picture. If you focus on each facial feature you may find it unappealing, but put together, they can make a pleasing sight.

This is true also in marriage. After a while, we stop seeing the entire picture and get caught up in the problems, imperfections, and faults. In all likelihood, they are probably insignificant in the large scheme of things, but by our focusing on

> General George Washington asked a group of soldiers to define the difference between the terms "engagement" and "battle." "The engagement takes place before the wedding," they answered. "The battle — that comes later!"

them, they take on more gravity than necessary. One day you might even wake up and decide your marriage must be in trouble.

> "Dan is a mess; he is terribly forgetful," the CEO told his wife. "It's a wonder he can sell anything."
>
> The next day the CEO asked Dan to pick up a salad for him on his way back from meeting with a client. But when Dan returned, he was very excited.
>
> "Guess what?" he said. "I made a great sale. The client agreed to buy a million dollars' worth of our product!"
>
> "So you forgot my salad?" the CEO snapped.

Familiarity Breeds Contempt

LOOK AT HOW IRONIC this is. We meet our mate, and all we are able to see are this person's positive qualities. After the wedding, we begin to focus on the negative. What's wrong with us? How is it possible that until the wedding all we sang were praises, and since then we find reason to complain and criticize.

It's not unusual that when you spend a lot of time with another person you start to see the person's flaws. Just as we tend to focus on our imperfections because we take ourselves for granted, it's natural to start taking our spouse, who has become so familiar to us, for granted.

There is a simple psychological reason for this. Prior to marriage, the couple is perfectly aware that this relationship, as solid as it seems, is very fragile. All it takes is one argument and the engagement can be called off. Both partners naturally make a greater effort to keep things flowing smoothly. If there is a disagreement, it is settled quickly.

After marriage, both parties feel they can relax. Calling it off will require a lot more effort, so they feel more secure about letting go and allowing the other person to see their negative traits.

Marriage vs. Divorce

She married him because he was very secure.	She divorced him because he was too full of himself.
He married her because she was so easygoing.	He divorced her because she was too docile.
She married him because he knew how to make a good living.	She divorced him because all he thought about was business.
He married her because she reminded him of his mother.	He divorced her because she was too domineering like his mother.
He married her because she was stable and calm.	He divorced her because she was monotonous and boring.
She married him because he was lively.	She divorced him because all he wanted to do was party.

Also, there's a tendency to think, *In the past, I made concessions and compromised more than I should have. Now it's my spouse's turn.* The same giving person that you were engaged to suddenly stops being so giving once married, expecting to now be "paid back" for all that benevolence. The problem is, of course, that when the couple stops putting in the same effort that they put into the relationship before the marriage, things start to fall apart. Each begins to focus on the other's flaws. Accusations and complaints begin to fly.

The Culprits: The P's and the A's

THIS IS WHERE THE P's and the A's play a part. For many, it is the pursuit of the P's and A's that keep a couple together in the beginning. The man looks for Prestige, Power, and Pleasure to make him happy. The woman looks for Affection, Appearance, and Accomplishment. These are things they look for in a marriage partner, whether consciously or subconsciously: someone who will fulfill these needs.

If you are a man, one of the reasons you married your wife is because you find her attractive and you enjoy her respect and adoration. This fulfills your need for Prestige, Power, and Pleasure in some way. As long as she fulfills these needs, you will respond by giving her attention, fulfilling her need for Affection.

After marriage, when the luster begins to wear off, couples begin to see each other's flaws and it can all go downhill. It's impossible to remain perfect all the time. She won't always look attractive, he may sometimes be in a bad mood, dinner may be late occasionally, he/she may not always be willing to give her/him space. So he becomes less responsive and shows her less affection. They become dissatisfied and begin to focus on the negative. Conflicts arise.

Soon there is more complaining and criticizing than appreciating and caring. It's as if they forgot why they married each other in the first place!

Maintain the Magic

THE OBVIOUS SOLUTION IS not to let go — to sustain the effort you put into the relationship before the marriage. Of course, it's easier to put in that effort when you see your fiancé once a week over dinner. How do you "maintain the magic" of the engagement when you are living with the person, picking up after him, and sometimes seeing her in less-than-ideal circumstances?

This is when the principle of "true love" is so crucial.[1] Your objective is to make her or him content. Look for ways to please your spouse (the suggestions in the previous chapter are a good start) and make your spouse feel unique and special. Focus on your spouse's good qualities, shower compliments, cards, or gifts on your spouse — do something that you know will send this message unequivocally.

It's helpful to remember that you are not two entities. According to Jewish mysticism, you are both halves of the same soul. When you achieve the realization that your spouse and you are one, it will be easier to fulfill his or her wishes even if they go against your personal preferences.

> "Happily ever after" means that two people find wholeness in each other. The loyalty they feel for one another comes from the fact that, primarily, they exist for each other.
>
> Each of us needs to experience the pain of halfness in order to get married. Without feeling our own halfness, we aren't able to let someone else into our lives. We need to feel that we really are half and not whole; and that by remaining alone, we'll never be whole.[2]

A young boy (who later became the sixth Lubavitcher Rebbe)[3]

---

1. See Chapter 8, "Love Is Not an Accident."

2. Friedman, *Doesn't Anyone Blush Anymore?*, p. 30.

3. Rabbi Yosef Yitzchak Schneerson (1880–1950). Challenged the Communist regime relentlessly to keep Judaism alive in Communist Russia.

asked his father, "Why did G-d create us with one nose and one mouth but two eyes?"

"With the right eye," his father said, "we must see the good in others. With the left, we should examine ourselves." The right eye is a metaphor for the things we do with fervor: Always look for the positive in others — especially your spouse. With the left eye, look at your own faults and see how you need to change and become a better person.

Unfortunately, many people do just the opposite. They use the right eye to look at everything that is wrong with the people they live with — especially their spouse — and they use the left eye to justify their own negative behavior.

A woman once entered my office and very emphatically stated, "I want a divorce. This is not negotiable. I have made my decision, and I didn't come to ask for your advice. What do I need to do?"

"Give me a couple of days and we'll talk," I replied.

I called her husband to get his take on the situation. "My wife feels that I'm irresponsible," he told me. "We just moved here from Bogota, and our immigration papers and legal status are in limbo. She is not willing to accept the fact that this is totally out of my control."

One week later, his wife began to have serious back pains. Her doctors recommended surgery, which took place shortly afterward. The husband did everything he could to assist his wife and be there for her. As you can guess, they never divorced.

What happened? People lose perspective and stop appreciating the good that their spouse does for them. They take it for granted and pick on each other's flaws, even things that they can't do anything about. When this woman realized that her husband was there for her, she was able to put things in perspective. True, he had imperfections and she didn't like some of his personality traits. But he had many qualities that she had overlooked. How ironic that G-d had to send her a back problem in order to salvage her marriage.

Don't wait until things get out of hand. Make it a practice to look for positive traits in your spouse. Focus on the good qualities and avoid seeing the negative. (Obviously, this does not include situations in which there is danger involved or if a spouse is abusive or mentally ill.)

The Bible tells us that one day, one of Noah's sons entered the tent where Noah was sleeping and saw that his father was naked. When he came out, he told the other brothers. The other two brothers entered the tent, covered their father, "and their father's nakedness they did not see" (Genesis 9:22–23). They saw that he needed to be covered.

If someone is uncovered, you simply go and cover him. You see what needs to be done, but you don't look for faults. You might see the condition, but you don't judge the person. Noah's sons didn't see nakedness in their father.

If there is something your husband or wife doesn't want you to notice, you don't look. You don't think, "I see my spouse's faults, but I'll bite my tongue and not say anything." That's not going to last long, and you'll end up with a bloody tongue.

The happier thought is, "I know my spouse isn't perfect, but I don't notice anything wrong. I'm not being a martyr; I'm not putting up with anything. I'm not long-suffering. I like what he or she is."

The reason you don't notice is not because you're so kind, so wise, and magnanimous that you overlook your spouse's faults. It's not overlooking; it's having respect for your mate's privacy.[4]

One time, a man returned home after work and found that everything was in complete disarray. The living and dining rooms were full of books. Potato chips had spilled all over the

4. Ibid., p. 7.

floor. Gum was stuck to the carpet. Lego was strewn every-where. He entered the kitchen to find food all over the place. The sink was full of dirty dishes and the garbage can was over-flowing. As he neared the bathroom he saw an avalanche of dirty laundry and towels. Then he walked into the bedroom. His wife was in there, reading a book.

"What's up?" he asked.

"Nothing," she replied nonchalantly. "In the past, you've asked me what I do all day. Well, today I decided not to do it."

Humility Is the Key

HOW CAN WE TRAIN ourselves to see the positive in our spouses?

One way is to ask yourself, *Where did all of my wealth, glamour, popularity, skill, and personal and professional success come from?* All these things are gifts that we have received from others — from our parents and grandparents, mentors, and primarily from G-d. So no matter how much you have going for you, there is no reason for you to be arrogant! Once again we need to remember that practicing humility is the key to appreciating the good in others.

There's another way to keep one's pride in check, and that is to contemplate the first leader of the Jewish nation. The Torah testi-fies that "the man Moshe was more humble than all men who lived on the face of the earth."[5] The Chassidic masters explain[6] how Moshe, who was the Jewish nation's greatest leader, who brought them out of Egypt and was the greatest prophet who ever lived, could also be the most humble. Moshe figured that if another person were gifted with his capabilities, that person

---

5. Numbers 12:3.

6. R. Menachem Mendel Schneerson, *Sefer HaMa'amarim* (5710), p. 236.

would have accomplished even more. Realizing that if someone else had our qualities, he or she would have exceeded our accomplishments, helps us keep our egos in check.

Arrogance is one of the great impediments to a healthy relationship because an arrogant person expects others to have the same qualities he does. He can't imagine that other people might find those things difficult or have limitations in those areas. If the person is organized, neat, and regimented, his or her spouse must be also be organized and neat. Arrogant people may even admit to having faults, but they can't tolerate these same faults in others. "If I am careless, forgetful, or lazy, that is acceptable, but not for my spouse. How can *I* be married to an imperfect spouse?"

When one of my congregants separated from her spouse, I asked her why.

"He is not the man that I envisioned I'd marry," she replied.

"Is he a good person?" I asked.

"Yes," she answered.

"A hard worker?"

"Yes," she said, "but he is not the husband I want."

Several months later, I heard that they reunited. I asked her what had changed.

"I realized that although he doesn't have all the qualities I want, I really appreciate the ones he has."

This woman found the humility to discard her vision of the "perfect spouse" (which doesn't really exist anyway) and appreciate the husband she had.

Two Chinese men were walking down a road when they chanced upon a frog. "If you eat that frog," one of them said, "I'll give you a hundred dollars."

"No problem," his companion said and he quickly popped the frog into his mouth. Afterward, the man who had lost the bet said, "It's my turn now. You should offer me a hundred dollars if I eat that frog over there."

"It's a deal," his friend said.

So the first man ate the frog and recovered his money.

Later he asked his friend, "If I started the day with a hundred dollars, and I still have the hundred dollars, why did we have to go through all the trouble of eating two frogs?"

Why do couples and their kids have to go through the turmoil of separation only to decide that they should reunite? Wouldn't it have been better if they avoided all the emotional turmoil, separation, and anxiety, and worked things out beforehand?

The answer is that people become stuck. They start to focus on the negative and get trapped. Sometimes it's only after they separate and have a chance to see things from a different perspective that they realize that the separation was needless.

Don't make the same mistake. Look for the good things in each other, compliment and praise each other, and you will avoid the heartache that criticism and negativity bring.

The Mishnah states,[7] "There were never greater days of joy in Israel than on the fifteenth of Av... On these days the daughters of Jerusalem would go out in white garments...and they would dance in the vineyards. The girls would say, 'Young man, lift up your eyes and see [the bride] you choose for yourself. But don't look for physical beauty; rather look at the family, for "grace is deceitful and beauty is vain, but a G-d-fearing woman shall be exalted."[8] The [young man] would reply [citing the next verse], 'Give her from the fruit of her hands and praise her actions at the gates.'"[9]

---

7. Talmud, *Ta'anis* 26b.
8. Proverbs 31:30.
9. Ibid. 31:31.

The Gemara[10] elaborates on this idea:

The pretty ones said, "Look for physical beauty, for the woman is unique because of her good looks."

The girls who came from respectable families said, "Look at the family, for a woman's uniqueness can be seen in the children she will have."

The plain-looking ones who came from common families would say, "Marry us for the sake of Heaven, but don't forget to give us gold jewelry."

These passages from the Mishnah and Gemara include many puzzling statements. For one thing, Judaism does not overemphasize beauty. The Mishnah itself says that "beauty is vain." So why does it mention beauty in the first place?

Secondly, the Mishnah states, "Look at the family," and the Gemara adds that this is because the woman's value is connected to her ability to provide children. What does this addition mean?

The Mishnah also adds a verse that seems unnecessary and ambiguous: "Praise her actions at the gates." What does this mean?

Finally, why do the plain-looking ones add, "Don't forget to give us gold jewelry"?

To answer these questions, we can say that the Mishnah and the Gemara are each referring to different things. The Mishnah focuses on the commitment aspect of marriage, and the Gemara discusses the groom's initial attraction and interest in his bride. Generally, a man chooses to marry a girl because of some quality that catches his interest. The Gemara therefore mentions the elements that initially attract a man: appearance and family.

---

10. Talmud, *Ta'anit* 31a.

Yet for the marriage to last, there must be a stronger commitment. This is what the Mishnah means when it emphasizes, "Don't get caught up in the external factors such as beauty." It adds the verse "Praise her actions at the end to advise the groom to make sure to compliment and praise his wife's actions." This will ensure a long-lasting marriage. The reason that the plain-looking girls ask for gold jewelry is to show that even if a woman is not beautiful, her appearance can be enhanced with jewelry and still attract a groom.

An arrogant and selfish person tends to focus on others' flaws.
This is the antithesis of what makes a good marriage.
Instead, train yourself to see the positive qualities in your spouse;
develop humility and be a giving partner so that you will be able
to appreciate his or her good qualities and overlook the flaws.

14 Can You Really Change Your Spouse?

THE DAY YOU MARRIED, the campaign began. Now, finally, you could get him to stop biting his nails and wearing jackets a size too big. You could finally tell him that you hated it when he sent food back to the kitchen in a restaurant, and he definitely wasn't going to be the husband who throws his dirty socks on the floor.

Some people enter marriage thinking that even if they don't like some things about their spouse, they can change them. Or maybe they liked everything about their partner when they married, but after marriage, they realized that their spouse wasn't as perfect as they thought. They began to see the flaws and thus began the campaign to improve them.

Is this realistic? Can you really change your spouse's personality or ingrained behavior?

Different Strokes

EVERYONE IS CREATED DIFFERENT. The Talmud puts it like this: "Just as their faces are different [i.e., humans don't look alike], so

146

their opinions are different."[1] This is also true regarding people's natures and personalities.[2]

Accepting that everyone is different is the foundation of a successful marriage. Intellectually we know that this is true, and we tend to accept this concept quite naturally — until we need to deal with it head-on. Whether it is a spouse, a child, or even a coworker, it's difficult to relate on a daily basis to someone who's on a different plane.

What happens when a man who prides himself on organization marries a woman who is, at best, laid-back about neatness? When he comes home, he expects to find the house in tiptop shape, the toys and shoes in their proper places, dinner ready, the table set, and the food fresh and hot. What he actually encounters are papers scattered around everywhere, shopping bags on the

---

1. Talmud, *Sanhedrin* 38a.

2. According to our Sages (See *Likutei Torah, Behaalotcha.*), the Menorah represents the entire Jewish people. The seven branches symbolize seven different types of Jews. Some are extroverted; others are introverted. There are individuals who are proactive and others who are passive.

The seven types of Jews represent seven attributes: love and kindness (*chesed*); vigor and discipline (*gevurah*); beauty, harmony, compassion (*tiferet*); victory, endurance, determination (*netzach*); humility and devotion (*hod*); foundation, bonding, connection (*yesod*); majesty and dignity (*malchut*). Each individual may possess a trace of all these attributes, but one trait is usually dominant.

In Judaism, we often refer to the famous schools of Beit Hillel and Beit Shammai. (The Torah academies founded by Hillel and Shammai around the first century were known as the "houses" of Hillel and Shammai. The Mishnah records 316 disagreements between the House of Hillel and the House of Shammai. The House of Hillel generally takes the lenient approach and the House of Shammai the more stringent one. In all but eighteen cases, the *halachah* rules in accordance with the House of Hillel.) Jewish mysticism explains that their philosophical positions reflected the composition of their souls. Hillel was primarily connected to the attribute of *chesed*, kindness. In Shammai, the attribute of *gevurah*, strength, dominated.

These traits are inborn and almost impossible to change. Instead, a person is supposed to channel his trait to achieve his potential in his own unique way.

couch, a supper that is still not ready, and unfolded laundry piled on the bed. The first time this happens, he calmly mentions to his wife that he's uncomfortable with the mess, that he prefers order. The second time he repeats his request in the sweetest of terms. By the third time, he is upset and frustrated. He can't fathom why his wife can't get it right. Can you imagine how the message will now be delivered? When we are upset, even the most important and heartfelt messages will be conveyed with contempt.

> A synagogue member once confided to his rabbi, "Ever since we got married, my wife has tried to change me. She got me to exercise daily, improve my diet, and stop smoking. She taught me how to dress well and enjoy the fine arts. She introduced me to gourmet cooking, classical music, and the stock market. But between you and me, Rabbi, I'm thinking of divorcing her. She just isn't good enough for me anymore."

What's really taking place? To the organized person, living in an organized manner is more than a way of life; it's a religion. He expects his partner to have similar values. He can't digest the possibility of being married to a slob. This makes him frustrated. The truth is, the disorganized wife isn't doing it on purpose; most likely she doesn't know how to be neater, even if she wants to. But instead of explaining how his spouse might become more organized, her husband, upset and frustrated, only conveys his discontent. This just exacerbates the problem.

I once met a couple who was going through some hard times. They fit the mold I just described. The husband was organized and insisted that the home always be tidy. His wife was not such a perfectionist. Eventually the husband began pestering his wife to be more neat. The wife not only was unable to accomplish this, but she felt constantly rejected. This left her feeling stressed about their relationship. And the home stayed messy.

The unorganized spouse didn't choose this way of life. In fact, she, too, would have preferred an organized home. She just didn't know how to do it. Things got out of control — the house grew messier and her spouse grew more dissatisfied — and she felt trapped in a vicious cycle. What she needed from her spouse was encouragement and guidance, not criticism.

Instead of stressing over the situation, he would have been better off helping his wife become more organized in a way that she could handle. Just telling her to be more organized accomplished nothing, because she didn't know how to do it on her own.

One of the greatest challenges I have ever encountered was trying to help a person who was convinced that he was 100 percent right. It was an uphill battle. Once the individual made a decision, everything just confirmed his point!

A woman told me she was frustrated with her husband because he was not involved with the children. After inquiring, I realized that he was spending more time with his kids than most fathers in his community. This didn't make a difference. His wife was convinced that he was not sharing the responsibilities! Exploring this case a little deeper, I noticed that her image of the ideal husband was very different from his reality.

Once we conclude that our mate is not the type of person we envisioned we would marry — and we insist that they have to change — the relationship tends to crumble.

There is a well-known saying, "My mind is made up. Don't confuse me with the facts." Although not to the same degree, this happens with many couples.

Marriage begins, and inevitably in the process of adapting to each other, we get bruised. We unintentionally hurt our spouse. This is a learning experience. Some are able to trek through this tough terrain and learn to appreciate how they overcame it. Others succumb: they can't see past the mist that obscures the way and they give up.

Men vs. Women

ACCEPTING EACH OTHER'S DIFFERENCES applies not only to character traits. It also means accepting that *men and women are different.* This is the whole premise behind the principle of the three A's and the three P's. Men don't look for the same things as women to make them happy. They pursue the three P's and women pursue the three A's — and this means that they react differently to the same situation because their needs and perspectives are different.

Once you accept that men and women look for different things in life, it is much easier for you to accept your spouse's behavior. A man who comes home from a day's work and locks himself in the den for an hour is only looking to unwind after a long day's work; it's not necessarily a sign that he doesn't like his wife's company! A woman who complains that her husband doesn't spend enough time with her isn't denying that he is a good provider; she just wishes that some of the time he spends in the office would be spent with her.

Obviously each spouse will try to put his or her own needs aside for the other, but denying that these differences exist leads only to trouble.

The differences between men and women should not be an excuse to give up on the marriage. On the contrary, this is precisely how G-d made us, and it is part and parcel of the marital relationship. In fact, when we work on bridging these differences to strengthen our bond, we make our marriages strong and fulfilling.

The Whole Package

THE TRUTH IS, WE have to back up and look at our spouse as a package deal. Both parties need to accept their mates as they are — the good, the bad, and the ugly. Neither you nor your other half were forced to marry. But after the fact, you can't choose the part you appreciate and reject the part you don't like. You need to accept the complete person.

If you accept this, then with patience and intelligence, you, together with your spouse, can work to improve (not change) *some* of your spouse's habits. The process can take months and even years. You may never achieve 100 percent success, but things will improve. More importantly, you will maintain a good relationship and a happy marriage.

> The fact that your spouse isn't perfect shouldn't be your problem. If your husband or wife were perfect, then you wouldn't need any talent or wisdom. The [goal] is [to acknowledge] that this person isn't perfect and it doesn't bother you. It's not your problem because you accept your spouse unconditionally. We are not talking about dangerous misbehavior or physical violence, just normal, human imperfections… It's not enough simply to tolerate your spouse's faults.[3]

The story is told about the robber who went to a rabbi and said, "Tell me how I can repent."

Rabbi: "What was your sin?"

Robber: "I stole a string."

Rabbi: "That is a sin, but if you return the string that will be sufficient."

Robber: "Yes, Rabbi, but the string was tied to a rope."

Rabbi: "In that case, return the rope."

Robber: "The rope was attached to reins."

Rabbi: "Return the reins also."

Robber: "They were connected to horses."

Rabbi: "What were the horses schlepping?"

Robber: "A wagon full of merchandise."

---

3. Friedman, *Doesn't Anyone Blush Anymore?*, pp. 6–7.

When you get married you are now connected to the entire package. You can't take the string without the wagon that's attached to it.

Practically speaking, you don't have to fight every battle yourself. If your spouse is disorganized and you value a neat home, for example, you can hire a cleaning lady for a few hours a day or a live-in maid if you can afford one. Or, maybe your spouse would enjoy taking classes on organization or working with a professional home organizer. The point is, be proactive, not reactive.

> An expert in time management was delivering a speech. He began by saying, "Whatever you learn here, please don't try it at home."
>
> He gave a brilliant discourse and received a standing ovation for his insight and clarity. In the question-and-answer period, someone asked, "Why shouldn't we try these techniques at home?"
>
> "After I got married," the lecturer replied, "my wife would prepare breakfast and it took about seventeen minutes. I explained to her how it could be done in eight minutes."
>
> "That's great!" the man in the audience responded. "So what's the problem?"
>
> "Before, *she* was making breakfast," the expert answered. "Now I am!"

Acceptance, Not Aggression

I HAVE A POOR short-term memory. It's hard for me to remember everything I am supposed to do. This can be very frustrating at times. For example, when I go shopping, chances are I'll forget to do another errand nearby and I'll need to return a second time. This is not very amusing. But I have come to terms with this deficiency.

Yet how many times can I expect my spouse to put up with this, especially when it affects her? My wife might call me at the office and say, "Hi, Ari, could you bring home the book on marriage you have in the office?"

"Of course," I reply.

After hanging up, I get busy with something else, and by the time I leave for home I've completely forgotten about the book.

After dinner, she asks, "Ari, do you have the book?"

"Oh. I forgot. I will bring it tomorrow."

Of course, the same scenario repeats itself the next day and then again on the third day. What should my wife's natural reaction be? Frustration? Anger? Annoyance? Irritation? She certainly would be justified in expressing her resentment, in telling me how she feels totally ignored and disrespected. But what would venting her emotions at me accomplish?

My defense mechanism would kick in and I would think, *Obviously I didn't mean to forget the book, and I haven't found a system to help me be more responsible, so why is she scolding me?* If it happened to be a particularly stressful day, I might respond, "Maybe you should get it yourself," or, "You always remind me at the wrong moment," or, "You also forget things." I doubt I would say, "You are right. I couldn't care less about you and I'm an irresponsible good-for-nothing."

To her credit and my luck, my wife is usually calm and understanding. In this case, she didn't chastise me. Instead, she asked me again to remember tomorrow. By now I felt bad. It really wasn't fair to my wife that I was so forgetful, so I had to come up with a plan. And I did. The next time she wanted something from the synagogue, I immediately found the item and placed it on my desk. You might think, *Now we're getting somewhere! You've found a way to solve the problem.* You are almost right.

Typically, I forgot the book on my desk! So then I began punishing myself for my forgetfulness and would go all the way back to the office if I forgot something. Nowadays, to avoid wasting time, I put my car keys on the item (somehow I never forget those) or just put it in the car right away.

So although I have a problem, my spouse's patience and understanding have pushed me to change. I'm convinced that if she had reacted angrily or aggressively, the results would have been disastrous.

> What's the best way to remember your wife's birthday?
>   Forget it once.

To a certain extent, we're all guilty of not accepting our spouse as they are. We are so concerned about changing them that they feel that a part of them is not loved. It's difficult to feel beloved and despised at the same time. Suppose a friend says, "You are a gentle man with a good heart, but I have a hard time believing how stupidly you act sometimes!" Can you or I truly maintain a deep friendship with such a person? Isn't the message we are sharing with our spouse essentially the same?

If you sincerely care about your spouse, why are you harming their emotional well-being while you are trying to get them to improve their physical health? Let's be honest. You want a thinner spouse, an organized wife, a husband who has more common sense, a person who is focused on the home, a spouse who has more family values… because *it would make your life better*.

These are our personal desires for our personal benefit. I don't mean to say that these things are not important, but if you are only expressing frustration and anger at your spouse's habits, your attitude and actions don't reflect a sincere concern for your spouse. You won't convince your spouse to change; you're convincing your spouse that you care only for yourself.

Rather than focus on the negative, you need to focus on the good. When people feel unconditional love, they will make an effort to change their habits. It's inconceivable that this will work any other way.

Books on raising kids all suggest that we need to show them that we love them just the way they are. Only then can we help our kids grow, mature, and change. Children should never, ever feel that your love is conditional — that only if you are smart, good, and responsible will I love you. This applies just as much to your relationship with your spouse.

Don't confuse a person's character with his or her achievements. What they do is not who they are. They may have limitations in a certain area or not always do things the way you would like, but that doesn't mean they don't deserve your love and commitment.

A Rebbe once asked his grandchild, "Where is Zeidy?"

The child pointed at his grandfather's hand.

The Rebbe shook his head. "This is Zeidy's hand," he explained. "Where is Zeidy?"

The child pointed at his grandfather's body.

"This is Zeidy's body," he said. "But is that Zeidy?"

Later his grandfather got up and the child called to him, "Zeidy!"

Smiling with pride, his grandfather turned around and said, "Yes! This is Zeidy."

Everyone has good qualities and imperfections. You can't take the good qualities and disregard the flaws — they are a package deal. Don't disqualify a person because of his faults; his faults don't define who he is. Once you can accept this, and accept the person you have married, flaws and all, then your spouse will be more open to change. He will know that you genuinely care about him — all of him — and you have his best interests in mind.

Don't attempt to change your spouse — this can destroy a relationship. If you can't accept your spouse for who he or she is, you can't expect your spouse to want to change. Acceptance and gratitude will take you much further than resentment and anger.

15 Bridging the Differences

IN THE PREVIOUS CHAPTER, we talked about accepting our spouses for who they are, flaws and all. If we accept them, they will start to change because they care about us and want to make us happy.

But what if these differences are more than just personality traits? What if the chasm between you is more vast? How can you learn to relate to a spouse who seems to be from a completely different planet?

> One day a woman pointed out a couple to her husband and said, "Look at them. They seem to be happily married."
> "Don't be too sure," he answered. "They're probably saying the same about us."

When G-d first appeared to our patriarch Avraham, He commanded him to leave home. This was to be one of the ten trials that Avraham would undergo. The wording used in the verse is intriguing, "*Lech lecha méartzecha umimoladetecha umibeit avicha* — Leave your land and your birthplace and your father's home…"[1]

Why was it necessary to enumerate all these details? Didn't

---

1. Genesis 12:1.

the commandment to leave "your land" include "your birthplace" and "your father's home"?

According to one explanation,[2] the Torah is teaching that we need to shed different habits and behaviors, and each level is more difficult to leave behind. We are influenced to a certain extent by our native country. We are influenced to a greater extent by our birthplace. But our home exerts the greatest influence of all. To begin a relationship with G-d, Avraham had to make certain that his past, in an environment of wicked people, would not affect his future commitment.

This idea applies to our marriage relationship as well. For the marriage to succeed, we need to ensure that our background and previous lifestyle does not conflict with our new endeavor.

Culture Clash

THERE IS NO DOUBT that people are influenced by the country in which they grow up. Note that the first order that Avraham received from G-d was "leave your land" — our philosophies, likes and dislikes, and other choices are affected by the culture in which we were raised. If you were born in Latin America, you will probably enjoy soccer more than baseball. If you are from Japan, rice will be an integral part of your diet, while in Mexico it will be tacos and frijoles.

Your native culture also affects your mannerisms and value systems. Even if you were brought up with the same religious values as your spouse, your surroundings have a strong impact on your way of life. You have various opinions about life because

---

2. See *Kli Yakar* on Genesis 12:1.

of the culture in which you were raised, and this will influence your approach toward marriage.

Men from Western societies, for instance, tend to be less controlling than men who were born in Middle Eastern countries. Women who were brought up in Western societies are usually more independent than women who grew up in the Middle East. A man with a Western-style background and philosophy should be able to achieve a fairly good relationship with a woman from the Middle East. But if a man from a Mediterranean background marries a woman from the West, their marriage will likely be more challenging.

> A rabbi told one of his congregants, "You're very fortunate that your wife comes from a Sephardic background."
>
> He meant that the man's wife was more likely to accept her husband's position as head of the home, while the typical Ashkenazi wife likes to run the show.
>
> "You're mistaken," the man said. "After we married, she turned into an Ashkenazi!"

In the Sephardic lifestyle, family and social life are very important. You marry not just an individual, you marry an entire family. You're expected to adapt to the extended family and relate to them as your biological family. When one is brought up this way, it's natural and normal, but if one is not accustomed to this system it can be overwhelming. In some cultures, men raise their voices to their wives and a shouting match evolves until they resolve the issue and then they go on with life. In other cultures, such an episode could destroy a marriage.

> Binyamin was visiting Israel and spent Shabbat with a family who had immigrated from Morocco. Kiddush was recited, the challah was eaten, and the meal began. The husband tasted

the fish, gave his wife a look, and said, "The fish is not spicy enough." He picked up the whole plate and threw it out of the window. He then tasted the hummus, made a face, and threw that plate out of the window.

Binyamin picked up his silverware and threw it out of the window. Perplexed, the host asked, "Why did you throw the silverware out of the window?"

"I thought we were eating outside."

I knew a couple who fought bitterly over their cultural differences. He was from the Middle East and she was European. The style of the country he was from is informal. The European style is very formal. This affected many areas of their life, including their eating habits, conversation, child-rearing, and recreational activities. The wife was convinced that her husband's casual demeanor would not be a good example for her children. They needed to be brought up the way that she was raised. Conversely, he disagreed with many of her decisions. This resulted in a series of disagreements and quarrels, which evolved into resentment and rejection. Each party believed the other was at fault.

One of the issues they fought about was table etiquette. He felt that it was okay to eat without a napkin over his lap. She was convinced that the children needed to learn proper manners. He thought it was okay if their kids spent less time on homework and received lower grades in exchange for spending time outdoors. To his wife, this was not an option. Putting the slippers next to the bed was acceptable in his mind. But it was clear to her that slippers needed to be in the closet. These were just a few of their many differences of opinion.

Such a marriage becomes very difficult to manage, especially when both spouses feel that they are the victims of intolerance and aggression.

"Why can't she tolerate my style?" he said.

"Why can't he accept that I know the true values that we need to transmit to the kids?" she said.

How can such a relationship continue to function? Their differences are ingrained in them and seem insurmountable.

If you have been making an effort to show true love to your spouse,[3] you know the answer. The premise needs to be, "Nothing has to be just the way I want it. Almost everything can be negotiated. It's not 'my way or the highway.'"

This is the first step — be aware of the effect culture has on your and your spouse's personalities and see how to deal with it.

Your Community

THE SECOND ORDER THAT G-d gave to Avraham was to leave his "birthplace" — what we might call the "community." The culture at large influences the foods you might like, dinner times, your vacation spots, and your general attitude toward masculine and feminine roles. Community values affect how you divide responsibilities, the type of job you have, and your role in the home. The community norms are even firmer and have a greater impact on the marriage than the surrounding culture. Who decides what to name the baby? Who decides which school the children will attend? How do you decide your priorities regarding spending and saving? Are both breadwinners or does the wife stay at home (or perhaps vice versa)? How do you manage your finances?

A couple I know divorced because they were from such different communities. A key factor in the breakdown of the relationship was that the husband came from a community in Israel

---

3. See Chapter 8, "Love Is Not an Accident."

where it is the norm for the women to work and help support the family. Naturally he assumed that his wife would earn money for the home. She, on the other hand, was brought up in a community where most women don't work. Sadly, they weren't able to resolve the issue and it led to their divorce.

Family Ties

BESIDES THE IMPACT OF the culture and the community, there is the most direct influence on a person: that of the family. You expect to have a marriage similar to your parents — that is, unless it was so terrible that you want to avoid anything like it. Either way, the family in which you grew up affects the family you build with your spouse.

Which of your parents paid the bills in your home — your mom or your dad? Who was in charge of the shopping? Was everyone expected to help in the house or did it all fall on your mother? Did your parents read to you at bedtime? How often did the kids get bathed — daily or weekly? Did your parents argue in public? Did one parent do all the talking? Was everyone demonstrably affectionate toward each other or were hugs and kisses rare?

Your pursuit of the P's or the A's may be affected by your upbringing. If you grew up in a more materialistic environment, you may feel a need for wealth and all that it brings — or perhaps you may have rejected this and decided you don't need to pursue wealth. If your mother was more reserved, you might not be aware of the importance of affection in a relationship.

These are among the challenges people face in marriage: the behavior and habits each spouse brings into their new home. Our primary experience with marriage is what we witnessed in our own homes while growing up. We come into our relationships with ideas and opinions that may be totally unfamiliar to our spouses, because our spouse was not brought up that way and may find these ideas hard to accept.

Who shops, washes the dishes, fills the car with gas, changes the light bulbs, locks the front door, picks up the dry cleaning, and runs the accounts? All these and many more responsibilities are common to every home, but the dynamics vary from family to family.

In London, my father-in-law was responsible for locking the front door at night. To my wife, the husband naturally has to be concerned about the safety and security of the family, so he is the one who bolts the door shut at night. In my home in Brooklyn there was no designated person. The last one in locked the door.

When we moved to Panama, my wife felt that this responsibility should be mine. I insisted that this law was not written in stone. One day I came in quite late, and as the last one home, I locked the door. My wife noticed that I had locked the door and said, "I'm happy you did that. I'm glad you did something for yourself."

Assuming she was thanking me for locking the door, I said, "But I did it for you."

She shook her head: "For me? You did it for yourself!"

"I'm telling you I did it for you."

"You must be kidding. I can't believe you're saying that."

By now I was very upset. *Why is she insisting on saying something that is totally untrue?*

This argument continued for a while. I pointed out that under no circumstances had I done it for myself. She insisted that she was right. You can imagine that we were each feeling offended by the other. More, I was mad at this totally uncalled-for, incoherent, and illogical assertion of my wife.

When we both calmed down and began to talk, I said, "It's hard for me to comprehend your claim that locking the door was for my own good and not yours."

"I didn't say that."

"What do you mean you didn't say that?"

Seconds before another round could begin, she interjected,

"I was speaking about the fact that you went to the sauna." (A doctor had recommended that I go to a sauna for health reasons, and I had finally gotten around to going.)

How embarrassing. So much energy wasted on a simple misunderstanding. This could have been avoided if I had asked my wife for an explanation instead of jumping to conclusions.

> A husband asked his wife to go to the neighbors' home to see how they observed Pesach. She looked through the window and saw the husband screaming at his wife.
>
> "What did you see?" her husband asked her when she returned.
>
> The wife didn't respond.
>
> "I asked, what did you see?"
>
> Again, she kept quiet.
>
> Frustrated, he raised his voice and hollered, "WHAT...DID...YOU...SEE?"
>
> Thinking about the scene she'd just observed at the neighbors', she replied, "I can see you know already, so why are you asking?"

When the In-Laws Get Involved

THERE IS A MAJOR difference between family and the other two influences, culture and community. The influence of the family is not just something from your past. When you marry someone, you are also marrying their family. A person may leave the culture or community in which he grew up, but he can't just leave his family behind.

Most married people will tell you that dealing with the in-laws is a major issue in the marriage. In-laws can cause conflict between married couples, because each spouse often believes that the in-laws are manipulating the other spouse.

In communities where people get married young, this situation is common. The parents consider the newlyweds too young and inexperienced to make wise decisions. As a result, both sets of parents feel the need to guide their married children.

So the struggle begins. All parties involved are convinced that they are in the right. The parents on both sides want to make sure their child has a say and is able to voice it. Meanwhile, the spouses are battling to get the in-laws out of the picture.

Needless to say, this is unhealthy for a marriage. I often remind in-laws to "please stay clear of your child's marriage. Many marriages have been damaged as a result of the best of intentions." More than once I've been approached by an engaged couple who were distraught because the parents were applying undue pressure on one of them or the other. This can bring only unnecessary ill feelings between the young couple. Each one feels that he or she must defend the parents, and they end up fighting a battle that is not really theirs.

I tell these couples, "Don't worry about this fight. Your mistake was to think that it was acceptable that your parents got involved. Tell your parents that the rabbi has prohibited you from taking unnecessary advice from them, especially when this can create a conflict. They shouldn't get involved in what furniture to buy, where to live, who you should go to for dinner, and how you should run your lives." This takes a great burden off the couple. Even if the parents are convinced that they are right, they should not interfere with their children's marriage. If their children make mistakes — and they will make mistakes — the couple must be allowed to work things out on their own without their parents causing complications between them.

Finding Common Ground

ONCE YOU ARE AWARE of your differences, you can talk about the issues and make a plan for dealing with them. Expect that one or both of you will need to reach a compromise in various areas. But if your marriage is strong, and each spouse feels cared for and valued, you will be able to work things out.

If you find yourselves arguing with each other, it's also important to analyze what is at the core of the issue. People tend to argue and stress over situations that, with a little understanding, could be avoided. (Remember my story about locking the door?) And in a marriage where two people come from vastly different backgrounds, there can be a lot of misunderstandings. So when a situation arises that has you upset or frustrated, tell your spouse you would like to talk about it. Find a place and time where both of you can talk calmly and focus on each other. The conversation itself will help both of you comprehend what is going on and seek ways to deal with it together.

It's also vital to remember that every person has principles that are extremely important to them. These are areas they will have a difficult time negotiating — they can be illogical. Sometimes it's best to just accept your spouse's craziness. Who cares if your spouse likes to wash the sheets twice a week, or will use only a specific brand of toothpaste. As the saying goes, "Pick your battles."

Of course, things get really sticky when you argue about an issue that you both are adamant about and won't compromise on. When you come across such situations where there are no happy mediums, you might want to find a third party — a rabbi, counselor, friend, or mentor — who can guide you in finding the correct way to approach them and hopefully solve the issue.

Many couples come from different backgrounds.
If you and your spouse have cultural differences, it's important to find common ground. Don't let arguments that stem from these differences get out of hand; uncover the core of the issue and get guidance if necessary.

16 Anger and Criticism Can Destroy Any Marriage

I HAVEN'T TOUCHED ON ONE of the worst negative traits that can destroy any marriage: anger and its first cousin, criticism.

Everyone fights occasionally. Whether it's a serious issue that you need to resolve or you're just feeling stressed out, one thing is certain: Anger only makes it worse. Even just getting angry and not acting on it creates fear and distance. It is even more destructive when a person expresses anger verbally, not to mention physically.

> I definitely have the last word in any argument. Anything that follows is a new argument.

Love is the foundation of marriage,[1] and you can achieve this only by caring, sharing, promoting closeness, being empathetic to your spouse. Anger accomplishes just the opposite. The only thing you'll succeed in doing when you become angry is scaring away your

---

1. See Chapter 9, "The Marriage Pyramid."

spouse. There is no way a relationship can flourish in such an atmosphere.

In a healthy marriage, we seek to build each other's self-esteem — to be there for each other and support one another. Anger accomplishes the exact opposite.

Obviously, I am referring mainly to anger that is verbally expressed. Being angry is not a healthy state of mind and is also not spiritually condoned. But if you're able to contain your anger and calm yourself down, it won't destroy your marriage.[2]

It's expressing your rage and acting on your anger — screaming, insulting, giving the silent treatment, breaking things, and certainly abusive behavior — that is destructive.

Losing one's temper is something that should not happen in a marriage except in very unusual and grave instances (such as when someone's life was endangered as a result of the other person's negligence). The damage this can cause a marriage is obvious. If it happens in public, it's even more devastating.

> No matter how justified we might feel, anger is never a justification for bad behavior. But unless we recognize anger as unnecessary and detrimental to the well-being of our relationships, we will never learn to give it up, to let go of it entirely. It will go on ruining our life and ruining our ability to have and maintain intimate relationships.[3]

✍ Anger causes so much damage because the anger tampers with a person's ability to think rationally. A person who doesn't think clearly can be hurtful, and even violent, because he lacks

---

2. If you find, however, that you are perpetually angry, you may want to consult a professional to help you find the cause. Even if you manage to avoid taking out your anger on your family, it will manifest itself in other ways. It may have an effect on your health, for example, or prevent you from achieving your life goals.

3. Friedman, *Doesn't Anyone Blush Anymore?*, p. 42.

control of himself. A classic example is the phenomenon of "road rage."

Road rage happens when a person is cut off while driving and becomes so outraged that he physically attacks the offender. Can we fathom something so illogical? Of course the driver was inconsiderate, but does the victim have to react in such a dramatic, not to say dangerous, manner?

Even if the person who was cut off feels that his life was being put at risk, his response is way out of proportion. The reason he reacts that way is that he feels the other driver launched a personal attack — a declaration of war — even though it clearly wasn't personal. The person who cut him off didn't even know him. Obviously the person who was cut off allowed his ego to get in the way. Imagine how much more damaging it can be when the relationship *is* personal. When you feel attacked by a spouse, you can't be blamed for taking it personally, even if your spouse never intended to attack you. The results can be devastating.

Clearly, anger damages marital harmony. The arguments, conflicts, criticism, and screaming that result from anger eventually wear down a relationship. When the marriage becomes a battleground, it begins to self-destruct.

As soon as Jack walks in the door, he says to his wife, "Sara, quick, bring me the newspaper before it begins."

Sara promptly complies.

"Sara, hurry, bring me my slippers before it begins."

She goes instantly and gets them.

"Sarah, bring me a coffee right now before it begins."

Finally, Sara can't contain herself. "Before WHAT begins?!" she shouts in frustration.

"Oy vey," Jack says, "it just began."

Getting to the Root of the Matter

WHY DO WE FIGHT? Is it differences of opinion? Selfishness? Intolerance? Economic problems? Unshared interests? Conflicting values and ethics? Different backgrounds? Cultural issues? Family pressures? Unresolved childhood traumas?

There is some truth to all of these reasons, but the underlying cause is low self-esteem. Whether this manifests as an inferiority complex and emotional weakness or an inflated ego, the result is the same: Something the spouse said or did offended the person and triggered the reaction.

We were all born with a void. During our childhood, it is hoped that the adults around us provide what we need to build healthy, positive self-esteem. However, the reality is that many people feel inadequate. When someone, intentionally or not, makes us feel bad or inferior, we react aggressively.

Often this happens even with the trivial issues in life. The insignificant evolves into an authentic argument that needs to be settled just as much as a disagreement over important issues.

A friend of mine came to me with a crisis.

"Could you believe this?" he told me. "I told my family that I wanted to go to our beach house for the weekend. My older daughter said she preferred to stay in the city. The next day I spoke with her again and convinced her to come with us. Before I got home to tell my wife, my daughter told her, 'We're going to the beach for the weekend.'

"My wife got upset. How dare I make plans for the weekend with my daughter without consulting her?

"I don't understand it," he finished, shaking his head. "My wife knew this was the original plan and she'd agreed to it. Why did she get so angry?"

"You thought that after persuading your daughter, you didn't have to consult with your wife again," I explained to him. "Your wife felt that the new information should have come from you.

Since it came from your daughter, she felt ignored, hurt, and offended."

Perhaps if his wife had thought it through, she might have realized that her reaction was a bit exaggerated. What difference did it make who told her the plans, if she agreed to the plan in any case? But her ego was running the show, telling her that her husband had shown her disrespect by not informing her himself. This led to accusations, complaints and trouble in the marriage.

> A man walking on the beach observed a child picking up starfish and throwing them back into the water. There were thousands of starfish on the shore; the child would never finish. The man walked over to the child and said, "Don't you realize that your effort won't make a big difference?"
>
> The boy tossed another starfish into the sea and said, "It might not make a huge difference to you, but it will make all the difference in the world to that starfish!"

Cut the Criticism

ONE OF THE MAIN factors that triggers fights, arguments, and anger is criticism. People tend to offer criticism quite freely, directly and indirectly, and usually it is well-meant. People like to give criticism, but no one likes to be on the receiving end.

> Nothing creates such a wonderful home atmosphere as a husband who refrains from comments and criticism.[4]

We all know how much we despise when people mention our flaws. More often than not, it makes no difference how the

---

4. Arush, *The Garden of Peace*, p. 62.

message is transmitted to us. Our tolerance level for criticism is very low.

Why can't we handle it when someone points out our imperfections? Don't we sometimes tell others about their faults? Isn't it common for us to tell our children, friends, or coworkers what they need to do to improve? So what's the big deal when others do the same to us?

When we criticize people, we think it is the right thing to do. In fact, we feel we are doing them a favor. After all, the Torah commands us, "*Hoche'ach tochiach et amitecha* — You shall surely rebuke your neighbor."[5] So it's a mitzvah to point out other people's faults![6]

> Four good friends met regularly for coffee and talked about everything and anything. One day, one of them suggested they each share their faults.
>
> They all agreed and the first one said, "I have a drinking problem. Every night I drink until I drop."
>
> The second one said, "I love to gamble. It's something I can't control."
>
> Then the third one confessed. "I beat up my kids when they misbehave."
>
> The last one stood up and said, "I love to gossip, and boy do I have an earful to go tell people today!"

When we're on the other side, however, we feel attacked and respond emotionally. Intellectually, we understand that it can be beneficial when our weaknesses are identified; it can help us

---

5. Leviticus 19:17.

6. Actually, there are specific guidelines for rebuking others (including our children), and some say that today most of us are unable to give rebuke properly and should refrain from doing so.

improve ourselves. But instinctively, if we perceive that someone is out to hurt us, we counterattack.

It all comes down to the saying, "Others make mistakes. I make unavoidable errors."

> What's the difference between constructive criticism and destructive criticism?
>
> The criticism I give others is always constructive. The criticism others give me is always destructive.

From a practical as well as halachic standpoint, harsh criticism is to be avoided. The message gets across only when spoken in a warm, friendly way.[7]

We all recognize that we have imperfections, and we even admit to them at times, so why do we respond defensively when someone else points them out? Why should a petty comment or slight, no matter how well-intentioned, feel so significant?

Rabbi Manis Friedman explains that when a person acknowledges a fault, he is basically saying, "I am a good person with a fine personality. I just have one or two flaws. What can I say? I'm human."

When someone else points out that same fault, the thinking process goes like this: *They are telling me I have no value at all. It's as if this person is out to put me down and hurt me.* He feels attacked. And what does a person do when he feels attacked? He goes into fight-or-flight mode.

As trivial as the assault is, it's about me, my ego, my existence. When I acknowledge that I have a fault, I am saying that I am an

---

7. Feldman, *The River, the Kettle, and the Bird,* p. 53.

eight out of ten. I'm not perfect, but I'm basically fine. When I hear it from someone else, I feel like a zero. This is way too much for me.

> One time, two friends met for coffee.
>
> "Hey, Roger," one said. "You look downcast. What's going on?"
>
> "Well, to be honest," Roger answered, "I just lost ten million dollars in the stock market."
>
> "Oh my, that's terrible," his friend said. "You must feel awful!"
>
> "Yes, I do — especially since five thousand of it was mine!"

Is Our Perception the Reality?

SOMETIMES WE GET INSULTED when we perceive criticism of ourselves, even if we're not the ones being criticized. What do I mean by this?

A man once told his wife, "The housekeeper isn't hanging my pants the way I like." A week later, he repeated the complaint to his wife.

"I'll see what I can do," she said.

The third time he mentioned this problem, she got upset. "Enough already! I said I'd take care of it!"

The husband immediately retreated. "My complaint is about the housekeeper. Why are you getting so defensive?"

Obviously, he didn't understand that his wife felt in charge of the home. If something wasn't functioning, even if it wasn't directly her fault, it was ultimately her responsibility.

Here's another way to look at it. When a client complains about one of your salesmen, you don't say to yourself, *It's okay. He is not upset at me!* Ultimately, the salesmen reflect your company and you.

Let us illustrate this with another example. How would you

feel if you were driving down the street and a teenager suddenly walked in front of your car? You did not have to come to a sudden stop, but you had the right of way and you were forced to slow down.

Do you feel put out? Upset? Angry? Shocked?

How about if it was an eight-year-old girl? Do you have the same emotional response?

If you said no, why? What's the difference?

When the teen crossed the street, you felt as if this person deliberately acted against you. You had the right of way and he had the nerve to walk in front of you! But when an innocent child does the same, you don't feel that she did it to spite you.

We see that when we feel the action was intended against us, we get upset. Yet intellectually, we know that the teenager was not intentionally trying to upset us. He was just in his own world. Or maybe he was impatient and thought he could get across the street before we came. In the majority of the cases, nothing personal took place — the parties involved didn't even know each other — yet the driver convinced himself that he had been slighted.

This is very common in marriage. We tend to overreact to petty things. Because we feel slighted, we defend ourselves and end up with a conflict. But in marriage, the winner also loses. You can't win an argument by attacking your spouse and expect your relationship to flourish.

Abe walked into his house at eight o'clock one night. His wife, Leah, had expected him home at seven thirty.

Abe: "Hi, Leah, I'm home!"

Leah: "Hi, Abe. What happened? Why are you so late?"

Abe: "I got stuck in traffic."

Leah: "You said you would be here at seven-thirty."

Abe: "I said I was stuck in traffic."

Leah: "That's a poor excuse! You should have left the office earlier. You knew that I prepared dinner and the entire family was waiting for you."

Abe: "Excuse me, but I don't like these accusations. Sometimes there are circumstances that are beyond my control. You're treating me like I'm a little child who misbehaved, and I won't tolerate this attitude."

Leah: "Lower *your* voice; I don't like it when you talk to me this way. If you were considerate of your family, you would be here on time."

Abe: "My voice *was* calm and I *didn't* raise it, but now I *will*. This self-righteous stuff of yours, telling me I'm not considerate of the family, is over the top! Are you out of your senses?!"

Leah: "Stop screaming at me! How dare you insult me? You come home late, invent a poor excuse, create havoc in the home, and then have the gall to play the victim!"

Abe: "You are always right! You can do no wrong! Whenever we have a fight, it's my fault."

Leah: "In this case, that's for sure true! You could have called to tell me you were running late!"

Abe: "You want me to speak on the cell phone while I'm driving? You always berate me for that! Now you're saying I should have done it? Besides, I thought of calling you, but then I realized I couldn't — the battery was dead."

Obviously if this scene repeated itself very often, we would need to analyze it differently. But under normal circumstances, the problem was not the half-hour that Abe was delayed. It was that Leah felt slighted.

In her mind, Leah was not important to Abe. She felt like she was not a priority, so she accused him of being inconsiderate, untruthful, and unreliable. Her greatest proof was the fact that he didn't call. If he had called, the entire episode could have been avoided. Their failure to communicate resulted in a thirty-minute argument that scarred the relationship.

Why did she take this so personally?

Her feelings of inferiority led her to assume that her husband didn't respect her. If we give in to feelings of low self-esteem and ego, we are more prone to get aggravated with our spouse. When we are emotionally sensitive, we get offended easily. Then we go on the attack.

Abe's reaction to his wife's onslaught also comes down to ego. When she confronted him, he felt criticized and his natural reaction was to get angry. He didn't consider that his wife was only expressing her anxiety and concern; his first instinct was that she was criticizing him, and this led to a full-blown fight.

I once was talking to an acquaintance on the train. In the middle of our conversation, his phone rang. I heard him ask his wife, "Which movie should we go to?"

I heard her say, "I know the perfect one," and she gave the name.

"Maybe look for another one," he suggested.

"I was told that it's a very good movie," she insisted.

The conversation ended.

A couple of days later, I saw him again. I asked, "How was the movie?"

"We stayed home," he stated flatly.

"Why?" I asked.

"I got upset at my wife because she insisted that we go to one particular movie, so we stayed home."

To me this was out of place. I overheard the conversation. She didn't say anything offensive or abnormal, so why did he get offended?

The reason was that he perceived that she was too firm and inflexible, and consequently this made him feel inferior.

> Sometimes a conflict can be avoided by not responding in kind to a spouse's anger. When one spouse gets angry, the other often reciprocates without thinking, allowing a spark to flare into a raging fire.[8]

---

8. Jacobson, *Toward a Meaningful Life*, p. 53.

When the ego gets in the way, many conversations turn into a competition. Neither party is focused on the topic, but rather on the ego. This happens to all of us.

In these situations, there are no winners.

When a person has low self-esteem, the smallest criticism can be taken as a serious attack. Even if it wasn't meant as criticism, it may be perceived as criticism. This leads to anger and aggression, and the marriage self-destructs.

PART 3

The Art of Communication

17 Step 1: Conflict Management

THE PRIMARY REASON FOR conflicts is that we take things personally, and then we instinctively go on the defensive. Low self-esteem and too much ego lead to anger and aggression.

This means that to head off a conflict, the first thing you have to do is change your thinking process. When another person criticizes you or you perceive that someone is criticizing you, you have to replace thoughts like "My wife doesn't respect me," and "My spouse is saying that I'm worthless," with different thoughts.

How should direct your thoughts when you feel your spouse is attacking you?

One + One = One

FIRST AND FOREMOST, the competition aspect needs to be removed. It's not me against you. Can you figure out this riddle? When does one plus one equal one?

Did you guess?

The answer is: marriage.

You and your spouse are not two separate entities. You are one unit. Even though at times you may feel anything but united, accept that you and your spouse are really one being.

Husband: "Doctor, I'm having a very difficult time with my wife. We don't stop fighting. Every day we argue about the pettiest things."
Doctor: "From what you're telling me, it sounds like you're stressed. To get rid of your tension, I recommend that you jog ten miles a day. Do this and call me in a week."
Husband (one week later): "Doctor, I called to thank you. My wife and I managed to avoid fighting the entire week."
Doctor: "That's great! How did you do it?"
Husband: "What do you mean how? I'm seventy miles away from home."

The Talmud[1] explains the mitzvah, "Love your fellow man as yourself"[2] with an example: Just as one hand would not do any damage to the other, we need to feel the same about our fellow Jews. We are one entity and if one Jew hurts another, it is as if one hand is hurting the other.

All the more so when it comes to our marriage partner.

The *Zohar*[3] actually says this quite emphatically. When G-d declared His intention to make a woman, she was joined to Adam. G-d separated this hermaphrodite being into male and female. The same applies to all marriages. We all begin as one soul that has been divided in this world. Our objective is to reunite through marriage.

How can this be accomplished? How can we achieve such a difficult task?

---

1. *Yerushalmi, Nedarim* 9:5.
2. Leviticus 19:18.
3. *Zohar* 1 91b.

Your Soul Mate Is Your Helpmate

INSTEAD OF ALLOWING OUR natural differences and perspectives to create miscommunication, let us try to see how we complement each other. It would be foolish for a pilot to view the navigator as an adversary because they have different jobs. So, too, in every company, factory, industry, there are many different responsibilities. At times, they may seem to conflict with each other, but each is essential. "Research and Development" and "Budgeting" might seem to conflict with one another by their very natures, but both are crucial to the success of the company.

G-d blessed every marriage with a male and a female. We must not see them as two forces going in opposite directions, but rather, as energy that needs to be fused together.

I once heard an insightful explanation to a seemingly difficult passage in the Torah. G-d exclaims, "It is not good for man to be alone. I will make him an *ezer kenegdo* — literally, 'an assistant against him.'"[4]

The phrase "an assistant against him" sounds contradictory. I heard the following explanation to this verse from Rabbi Moshe Nidam: "If you feel that your wife has the opposite perspective and outlook, this is not negative; it's positive." While it may appear as if she is acting "against you," she is actually your "assistant." A person who agrees with everything you say is not necessarily helping you. Seeing a different angle helps you analyze and perfect your views.[5]

---

4. Genesis 2:18.

5. The Talmud states (*Ta'anit* 7a) that studying Torah alone is counterproductive. Only when you study with a partner can you be sure that you are not fooling yourself. The partner helps you see a new angle and so encourages both partners to prove their point of view or accept the other's argument. "*Umitalmidai yoter mikulam* — From my students I have learned more than from my teachers and colleagues," states the Talmud (ibid.). According to Rabbi Chaninah, his students' challenges forced him to attain a deeper understanding of the text.

The point is, by giving us an assistant who is "against" us, G-d gives us the chance to put our ego on the side for a moment. Then we can evaluate our spouse's perspective and decide which way is correct.

Winning Is Losing

IT'S TIME FOR A confession. When I got married, I had no concept of what marriage truly entailed. It was the norm for me to state my opinion on most issues without reservation. I was coming from the yeshivah world, a place where we would spend practically all day analyzing Talmudic text. Every day we would try to demonstrate that our understanding of the text was the accurate one. You can imagine that our minds were quite sharp. When it came to arguments with my wife, it wasn't a fair match.

At the beginning of our marriage, I was able to persuade my wife that I was correct in the majority of our conversations. This continued until, one day, I had a revelation.

My wife said, "You are able to convince me that you are right, but it's not making me feel any better."

From then on, I began to listen to my wife's point of view. Immediately, I was able to perceive the value of looking at things from a different perspective. It reached a point that, for a while, I was only listening to her opinion and not even considering mine! One of the wisest pieces of advice I received was from a close friend. He said, "My father told me to always remember that a wife is not a *chavruta*."

A *chavruta* is a study partner. When two people learn the same text, they tend to have different perspectives. The objective of the *chavruta* is to ensure that the two discuss and debate the issue until they reach a mutual agreement.

A person who is accustomed to this sort of give-and-take might encounter problems in his marriage. The usual reaction when confronted with a disputant is to show how your logic is superior. In marriage, this is negative and destructive. When your wife feels that everything has become a heated discussion, she will perceive that she is in a debating club, not a marriage. ⟩

When you win the battle in marriage, you almost always lose the war. This occurs even when the loser agrees that he or she was at fault. How about when the loser sees that he or she is no match for the other's way with words, but truly believes that he is in the right? Declaring victory in such a situation is complete nonsense.

Instead, we are better off acknowledging that we don't know everything and that we have areas in which we have to improve. Moreover, our spouse is given to us to help us with this endeavor.

When G-d put us in this world, He gave us the opportunity to perfect ourselves. Our resources and life circumstances are meant to help us in this life mission and we must choose to become a better person. This applies to every aspect of life. We are not supposed to follow our instincts and live only according to our nature. We are supposed to overcome our nature so that we can contribute to our society, and to our relationships, both our relationships with others and with G-d. This is part of the G-dly plan.

To do that, we need to activate our rational thinking processes rather than be led by our emotions and instincts.

Be Rational

OUR SAGES SAY THAT our *yetzer hara* (evil inclination) enters our body at birth, while our *yetzer tov* (good inclination) concludes entering when we reach the age of bar/bat mitzvah. It would seem that the opposite is true. Most of us associate small children with innocence and goodness, while adolescence seems to be a time when kids battle with hormones and a desire to get involved with negative influences.

The explanation is that our *yetzer tov* is the part of us that is connected to our rational, thinking processes. This is the aspect that permits us to change our nature and do things differently. By listening to our cognitive and rational side we can become better humans.

Up until our bar/bat mitzvah, we are basically functioning instinctively. Afterward, we begin learning how to use our intellect so that we can change. This does not happen suddenly or automatically, but we have now acquired the ability to do this.

And there is no better place to work on improving ourselves than at home with our own families.[6]

One night at about 10:00 p.m., a friend called. "I must speak with you," he said.

"Please, come right over," I told him.

He arrived within minutes and it was very obvious that he was angry. Very angry.

He had just had a big blow-up with his wife. Like a fire that ignited from a spark, the discussion had evolved into an argument, then a war between wills — his and hers. "I want a divorce," he exclaimed.

After a long conversation it seemed like he calmed down a bit, so I was hopeful. But then he again reiterated his intention in seeking a divorce. So now I decided to play my ace.

This man was religious, so I asked him, "Does your decision

---

6. The *kohen gadol* (high priest) had to be married to be eligible to perform the Temple service on Yom Kippur, the holiest day of the year. Why? This is obviously a biblical law that we must obey, whether we understand it or not, but Rashi suggests that a family is necessary for a person to truly feel compassion for others. Another possible reason is that the *kohen* had to have attained the trait of humility in order to beseech G-d's blessings. A person who is single doesn't have enough opportunities to reach this level. Only a married person who must take another individual into account can acquire the level of humility needed to be a proper representative for the Jewish people.

to divorce your wife come from your *yetzer tov* (good inclination) or your *yetzer hara* (evil inclination)?" In other words, was he thinking rationally or was he letting his emotions lead him?

"It's probably coming from my *yetzer hara*," he admitted.

"*Nu*," I said. "What do you think about that?"

"I think that this time I agree with my *yetzer hara!*" he retorted, trying to stifle a smile.

Thank G-d, the crisis had passed. He was calmer and able to go back to his wife and work things out.

G-d wants us to achieve marital harmony. When we have conflicts and troubles that cause our marriage to deteriorate, it is due to the forces of destruction that prefer a chaotic world. The *yetzer tov* — our rational aspect — is the part of us that we need to activate in our marriage relationship. It's our nature to pursue our own needs. But we are meant to use our rational thinking processes to consider the other person's needs and perspectives.

A young religious man got married the week before Pesach (Passover). That year, the young couple spent the *yom tov* (holiday) with the wife's family. All was going well. The *Seder* was quite enjoyable, the atmosphere jovial, the energy electrifying. Until the mother-in-law served the soup.

While the groom was eating his soup, he saw something floating on top. He bent closer and saw, to his horror, that it was a grain of wheat. A grain of wheat in hot soup would render the soup unfit for Pesach!

The groom went ballistic. How could his in-laws be so careless? He got up from the table and stormed out of the room. The family was distraught. How could this have happened? They always made the utmost effort to clean their home meticulously before the holiday. Everyone was doubly saddened because they had violated the laws of Pesach and they were concerned how this would affect the newlyweds' relationship.

The next day, the groom and the father of the bride went to the synagogue. The rabbi immediately recognized that something was not quite right. He approached the father of the bride and was told what happened.

When prayers were over, the rabbi invited the groom into his office to talk. The groom readily agreed. In fact, he was already considering asking for a divorce. After going over what had occurred to make sure the details were correct, the rabbi asked for the groom's *shtreimel* (fur hat). He gently turned it over and knocked it against the table several times. When the rabbi lifted the *shtreimel*, they both saw wheat grains on the rabbi's desk.

In those days, people would throw grains of wheat at the groom before the wedding as a way of blessing the couple to have a large family. It seemed that some of those grains had gotten stuck in the hat, and when the groom leaned over to eat his soup, one grain fell out.[7]

In marriage, we often blame the other person for our mistakes. But the reality is that they stem from us! It takes humility to accept that we're not perfect and realize that our spouses are there to help us perfect ourselves.

G-d created us with the objective of perfecting our souls. Every step of life's journey — the place we live, the job we do, the person we marry — plays a part in this plan.

> Our spouse is our helpmate. If we accept that a spouse is given to us to help us perfect ourselves, we won't feel attacked when they criticize us. We will listen with an open mind and take their opinion seriously.

7. Rabbi Paysach Krohn, *Around the Maggid's Table* (Mesorah Publications, 1989).

18 Step 2: It's Not What You Say, but How You Say It

I F YOU WERE ASKED who begins most of the quarrels in your marriage, chances are you'd say, "My spouse." How can it be that in most of our disputes we are the victims? It's impossible that everyone's spouse is always the aggressor. It would make more sense that in 50 percent of the fights I am at fault and in 50 percent you are at fault, or 70/30, but how can it be that both partners claim that 85 to 95 percent of the time it's the other one who initiated the fight?

The truth is that an argument has *two* sides: the initiator and the reactor. One spouse said or did something while the other reacted poorly. The first spouse responds in kind, and the other spouse retorts. Back and forth it goes, and before you know it, they are having a huge fight.

Dad: "I can't believe you kicked your brother in the stomach!"
Son: "I didn't mean to — he shouldn't have turned around."

Who started it?

One claims the other started it by reacting so aggressively to something he said or did. The second objects, saying the first one started it by launching the attack.

What can they do to stop this pattern?

Getting the Wrong Reaction

HOW DO YOU FEEL when you say something to someone and the other person replies pointedly, "Of course! That's so obvious."

That response makes you feel like a fool. In effect, the other person is telling you that what you said is common knowledge and it was unnecessary to even mention it. If you were smart, they are implying, you would know this.

When someone talks to you this way, it's not very pleasant and it's tempting to respond in kind, perhaps with a sarcastic remark or a defensive statement. Usually most people can brush off comments like this. They are annoying, but you'd rather avoid an argument than try to convince the other person of his or her insensitivity.

But what if the other person is a good friend or a spouse, and they are always making comments like this? Such remarks can lead to arguments, because it's hurtful when someone close to you acts insensitively or doesn't show you respect.

It would be better if they'd say nothing, or instead of saying, "That's so obvious!" say something like, "I think I've heard that before," or, "That's an interesting thought. It makes sense." The original comment, "Of course! That's so obvious!" is condescending. The suggested responses, on the other hand, convey respect, even if the message is the same.

Often, the rest of it's not *what* you say but *how* you say it that causes arguments.

You're probably thinking, *Of course! That's so obvious!*

As obvious as it sounds, it's surprising how so few people master this formula. Often we are so accustomed to talking in a particular way that we are unaware of precisely what we are saying and how we are saying it. This is the catalyst for many arguments.

I was counseling a couple with a troubled relationship. Every time I saw them we spoke about the exact same topic, and every time they would end up arguing. She would throw out an accusation, and he would respond aggressively. He acknowledged that his reactions were uncalled for, but he had a difficult time controlling himself, claiming that his wife provoked him. She, on the other hand, wasn't able to accept that he was reacting to the way she addressed the issues.

The way we speak will either start an argument or avoid it. It will initiate a confrontation or prevent it. When others sense that we are upset, they react in kind. On the other hand, when a request is communicated calmly, they are likely to respond in the same manner.

It is therefore a good idea to consider how you would communicate something to your spouse when you're not in the heat of emotion. Then, when you're upset, you might be able to pull out the right words. You'll find that choosing your words rather than letting out your frustration in the heat of the moment is more likely to evoke the response you are looking for.

When you make a request or express criticism, you might find it handy to use what's called the "sandwich method." This means "sandwiching" your request or criticism between two compliments.

For example, begin the conversation with a compliment like, "It's nice that dinner is always ready when I come home."

Then add your request, "I would appreciate it if you could pick up the dry cleaning on Thursday, so we don't need to rush on Friday afternoon."

Finish with another compliment, "I see you really try to please me," or, "I really appreciate how you take care of things promptly."

Not This but That

WHEN COMMUNICATING WITH YOUR spouse (or anyone, for that matter), you want to be aware of three things:

⊕ tone of voice;

⊕ body language; and

⊕ sentence structure.

Usually, the words you choose affect your tone of voice and body language. Can you imagine saying, "I would appreciate it if you would pick up your socks," with an angry tone and threatening body language? Even if you are saying something entirely innocent, if it is expressed in an aggressive tone of voice the other person will view it as an attack.

Let's consider some examples, and think about how we feel when someone criticizes us and how we'd like the person to say it differently.

How would you feel if someone said:

"Why did you park crooked?"

"Why are you so late?"

"Why did you leave the lights on?"

"Why did you leave the towel on the floor?"

"Why is the garbage still here?"

"Why are the kids failing in school?"

"Can't you be more organized?"

"Can't you be neat?"

"Can't you listen?"

"Can't you stop nagging?"

When you read these questions, how did you feel? Most people feel threatened, especially if the other person's angry tone of voice and tense body language contribute to the message.

Most of these issues are not unreasonable. It's perfectly all right to ask another person to be more organized, to stop nagging, to pick up the towel when finished with it, to take out the garbage, and to help the children succeed in school. The problem is that these requests are being issued as attacks. This way of speaking will not elicit the desired response. Instead it will provoke defensiveness, anger, and resentment.

Let's look at some alternative ways that the above questions could be phrased:

"I'd prefer it if you'd park closer to the curb. Otherwise, I worry that the car will get scratched by a passing car."

"I enjoy eating dinner as a family. Can you please try to be home on time?"

"Would you please turn off the lights?"

"Could you please pick up the towel from the floor?"

"I'd appreciate it if you'd take out the garbage."

"I think the kids could use some more help with their schoolwork. Can we talk about it?"

"I get frustrated when I can't find things. What can we do to get the house more organized?"

"I like it when you make an effort to be neat."

"I feel like you're not listening to me."

"I don't like the way you are talking to me. I know what you want me to do, and I'll get to it as soon as I can."

These sentences relay basically the same message as those above, but I bet your reaction to them was very different.

Notice that in the first set of requests, it's all about "you"; in the second, the focus is on "I" and "me." Instead of, "Can't *you* take out the garbage?" it's, "*I'd* appreciate it if you'd take out the garbage." Instead of, "Can't *you* listen?" it's, "*I* feel like you're not listening to *me*."

So instead of, "*You* are an irresponsible driver," say, "*I* would really appreciate it if you would drive slower or more cautiously."

Instead of, "Why are *you* so careless with our finances?" say, "It's really important for *me* to know that our finances are being handled properly."

Instead of, "It's obvious that *you* don't care about my feelings," d to know that my feelings are important to you."

mple difference between the two is that the former

n attack and the other sounds like a request or need.

ian implying that the latter person is at fault or lacking, you are saying, "I have a need that needs to be fulfilled."

Like Responds to Like

ONE OF MY FAVORITE examples that illustrates this idea is related to driving.

In Panama, men (including this writer) tend to drive quickly. We typically drive fast in and out of lanes and slow down only when we are practically on top of the car ahead. Whenever this happens, the wife bites her lip until she can't take it anymore.

"Careful!" she shouts. "Watch out!"

How does the driver respond? "Calm down!" he usually snaps back.

If this happens a second time during the drive, the wife will expresses herself again. "COULD YOU SLOW DOWN, FOR HEAVEN'S SAKE?"

The response comes immediately. "NEXT TIME, YOU DRIVE!"

Now let's change the players. This time a little child is sitting in the back seat. His father is driving the minivan like it was a sports car. The kid blurts out, "Daddy, careful. Watch out!"

Do you think that the father will use the same words and tone of voice that he used with his wife? Of course not. What will he do? He'll slow down. So why does he get upset when his wife says the same thing?

When my child raises his voice and says, "Watch out," it's clear that he is frightened. His reaction is not about me, it's about him. There are no explicit or implicit messages about my driving skills. My child is concerned and worried. As a good parent, I will slow down to help him feel safe and secure.

By contrast, my spouse's choice of words might be the same, but I assume that the intention is very different. When my wife tells me, "Watch out," I take it as "You are inconsiderate and irresponsible. Don't you see that you are putting our lives in danger?"

Is this what was really said? Directly, no; indirectly, yes. Like the child, the passenger is also scared. But coming from an adult, the implication is also that the person's life is being threatened by the way the driver is driving, and naturally the person must consider the driver reckless. The driver doesn't necessarily consider that those words stem from fear. It's more natural to take it as an attack.

In other words, my spouse is conveying two messages when she tells me to watch out (even if that's not what she intended), but I am hearing only one of them. What are the two messages?

1. I am frightened.

2. You are careless.

What do I perceive? I am being criticized. I don't consider that my spouse is speaking out of fear. Under these circumstances, my defense mechanism kicks in and I respond by opening fire.

Instead, if my wife uses "I" or "me" wording, she will be able to convey her fear, and I won't take it as an attack. "Please slow down. This makes me feel very anxious."

It's clear that our choice of words affects the reaction. If we can express our needs without implying that our spouse is imperfect or careless, we will be far more successful — and there will be notably fewer arguments.

We criticize when something was done or not done against our wishes. This results in an emotional state that may cause a person to say something he will later regret. An emotional rather than rational reaction actually diminishes the desired purpose of the criticism. When you must criticize, do so with your intellect rather than with your emotion.[1]

There is no doubt that a great number of disputes can be avoided if we apply this golden rule: Talk with your spouse, not at your spouse. Talking at your spouse is an attack; instead, help them understand what *you* are feeling.

Ask your spouse if he or she identifies with this idea. Try to analyze your last several disagreements and see if you can identify this pattern and think about how you can change it so you can avoid these arguments.

> The choice of words affects the reaction. An attack with words
> and tone of voice makes others feel threatened and they react
> in kind. Instead, speak in a soft tone and use "I" or "me."
> And don't forget "please" and "thank you."

---

1. Twerski, *The First Year of Marriage*, p. 59.

19 Step 3: Stop before You Start

I N THE LAST CHAPTER we discussed the importance of choosing the right words to avoid starting an argument. But what happens when your spouse slips and says the wrong words? They forgot to choose their wording carefully and modulate their tone of voice. Is that the end? Is the fight inevitable?

Not at all. Your reaction remains entirely your choice: whether to avoid a fight or to say something that will inevitably lead to one.

This Is War

WORDS OF WISDOM: THE best advice for someone who is under water is keep his mouth shut. Similarly, a conversation that is going badly needs to be cut off.

What usually takes place is we choose to go for the entire fifteen rounds or until the knockout. That's because once you counterattack, the discussion becomes a matter of ego and pride — it becomes an argument that requires a winner and a loser. The one who admits that he or she is wrong is the "loser."

> It takes a wise spouse to have the last word... and not use it.

Both parties feel that they must convince the other person

that they are right. Although they have yet to succeed in convincing their spouse, they think that this time around it will be different and they will prevail. *Once and for all he (or she) will have to surrender and accept that I am correct.* So it becomes a matter of, "I am in the right, and I am determined to fight to prove it. If I don't put my foot down, you will take advantage of me."

When we don't apply the brakes, we are in for a serious crash. Some couples I know get aggressive when the fighting starts, and go for the jugular. Each side must win at all costs. By the time the argument is over, they are on the verge of killing each other.

When a conversation becomes an all-out war, we don't even care what the discussion is about. We tend to ignore what the other person is saying altogether. We just focus on how to win the battle. All thoughts of marital harmony, of, "We're in this together," and finding solutions go out the window.

The smart spouse is able to step aside and doesn't get pulled into the dispute in the first place. Your spouse may have fired the first salvo, but if you fire back, you're just as guilty of starting the fight. Knowing when to stop the conversation will help you avoid its escalation. Or, to put it another way, the best way to get the last word in an argument is by saying, "You're right." Instantly the resentment and anger is defused, and suddenly you have opened the way to a calm discussion.

But while this sounds simple in theory, it's often difficult to implement.

So Many Opportunities...to Disagree

WHEN I GOT MARRIED, I was naive and innocent. I had no clue that marriage entailed dealing with some challenges. What could be so difficult? I had many friends, I was very sociable, so I figured that marriage would be an easy adjustment.

This was not the case. I soon realized that I was totally unaware of what married life was all about. My ego was frequently challenged. Sometimes our disagreements were a matter of culture; what I considered acceptable, my wife thought inconsiderate — and vice versa. In my perception, my partner was guilty of exaggeration. It even crossed my mind that she was trying to manipulate me (which, of course, was not the case).

I was baffled. I was the only son among a number of sisters, so I thought I knew everything about women. There would be no surprises. Then I learned that a sister is not a wife. There are similarities, but many differences. There were fewer territorial issues with my sisters. Since we didn't share bedrooms, we avoided issues of cleanliness and space. Positive reinforcement, which is so important for a couple, is not part of the day-to-day life of siblings. In addition, you don't have to consult your siblings to make important life decisions relating to children, home, bills, vacations, neighbors, budget, and hundreds of other subjects that are not applicable in a relationship amongst siblings.

What really perturbed me was that most of my disputes with my wife occurred not over the big life decisions, but over insignificant topics. Why did we argue over such petty matters? It bothered me that I took these arguments personally. What was the big deal if my wife asked me why I was late or criticized me for forgetting to do something? Was I so immature that I had to react over every small indication that my spouse was unhappy with my actions?

Occasionally this continues to trouble me, but I have come to terms with the fact that we are frail human beings. We might project strong characters, but our armor can easily be penetrated. Most people have very fragile self-esteem, and when they sense that they are under attack, they go into the offensive mode.

By applying the third step — stop talking — we can save ourselves an enormous amount of pain.

Stop It before It Starts

TYPICALLY, A DISAGREEMENT BEGINS with a small attack on the ego. The response also comes quite easily. Then the couple enters the, "I can answer back," mode. From there it goes into, "I can be just as nasty, if you wish." This is what inevitably happens if neither spouse stops the interaction in time.

Changing a tire is much easier than repairing a car that was totaled. If the conversation is stopped when there is just a little damage, there will be no need to rescue the car from a wreck.

This reminds me of a visit I made to a community member who had a difficult marriage. Both spouses had strong personalities and were stubborn. They were, I was told, often going head-to-head. After the husband explained the situation to me, I said, "Ben, why don't you apply this simple rule? When you feel that your wife says something you consider is offensive, just keep quiet."

"Rabbi," he replied, "that is exactly what I do. When she says something aggressive, I stop talking to her."

Before I could congratulate him or try to understand why the marriage still wasn't functioning, he added, "...for a month."

Our conversation ended right there. It was too much and I just laughed. But the truth is, of course, that it wasn't funny. This couple, like so many others, suffered from the "not being able to see life from another vantage point" syndrome. Each one could not understand how the other spouse didn't see how obviously right they were.

Imagine you are the CEO of a corporation, and your vice president is an exceptional entrepreneur. The success of the company is mainly due to his input and ideas. But he has a temper and once a week on Thursday, he throws a fit. What would you do? Get rid of him? Or ignore him on Thursday?

The secret to responding to a spouse who is in a bad mood or stressed is to stay out of the way. If your spouse has an emotional outburst once in a while, learn how to see the larger picture and don't get caught up in the explosions. Never make the mistake of taking it personally.

This doesn't mean you should ignore your spouse or disregard his or her feelings. It means that you shouldn't let the outburst put you on the defensive. Instead, when your spouse begins attacking you and telling you everything that's wrong with you since the day you were born, just duck. Under no circumstances should you get into the ring. Rather than counterattack, say, "This sounds important, but this is not a good time to discuss it. I am not ignoring you, but I don't want to fight. Let's find a time to talk about this later when we are both calmer."

> Once, a man was challenged to a duel. At the appointed time, his servant showed up and delivered the following message to his challenger, "I will be happy to take you up on your invitation to a duel. If I don't arrive on time, start without me."

If your spouse criticizes you, you still have a chance to prevent an argument: Instead of answering back, take a time-out and say that you will be willing to talk when you are both calmer.

20 Step 4: Mending Fences

WHILE I WAS IN the midst of writing this book, I met a couple who seemed to have a pretty good marriage. But when I looked beneath the surface, it was clear that their marriage was in trouble.

The problem was that one spouse was applying the rule of not answering back to an extreme. Whenever they had a disagreement, the husband would keep quiet and it would end there. While this method was successful in preventing arguments, the husband was unhappy. He felt that he had no voice in the home and that his wife always had things her way. All she had to do was have a tantrum and he would surrender. Slowly and steadily, his resentment built up and their relationship was negatively affected.

This is precisely why it is important to apply the third rule: Learn how to mend what was said.

The Delete-and-Remove to Trash Resentment Option

THE UNWANTED HAPPENS, EVEN to the best of us. When we are under stress, all our good intentions vanish and we end up fighting. Our words are confrontational and provocative, the response we get is offensive, and neither of us has the strength or courage to end the argument.

Now what do we do? After we burned the bridge, can we rebuild it?

Every married couple has gone through some event that caused them to wonder, "Now what?" It's hard for them to believe that after all that was said and done, they can rebuild the relationship. A bridge, once burned, is indeed hard to rebuild. One thing is sure: If friends argued like married couples, very few friendships would last.

What is the real difference between the two relationships? Why would a disagreement between two colleagues permanently finish their friendship, yet in marriage we are willing to carry on?

While I wish for "commitment" to be the correct answer, "personal interest" may be more accurate. The stakes are too high. We've invested too much to just close the enterprise. So we hold on and continue.

> "You know, David," said Jack to his friend, "I married my Sarah for her looks, but not the ones she's been giving me lately!"

But what about the argument? The hurt you caused to each other? Shouldn't you consider fixing the problem? Or is it better to just sweep it under the rug and move on?

Often this is exactly what couples do. Both parties fear that the fight will continue and lead to something that can't be undone. So they choose to swallow hard, be courteous, and act as if nothing happened. Some do this after an hour, and for others this takes a number of days, but eventually they move on.

For short-term marriages, this may work. But if you plan on staying married for many years, it is unhealthy and unsustainable. It's a time bomb. In the story I mentioned above, the couple didn't fight because one spouse refused to enter the fray, but he was slowly becoming resentful of his wife. This was eating away at the very fiber that kept the couple together.

A computer that is overloaded crashes. The more resentful we are, the more we keep inside of us, the greater the explosion and the more difficult the repair. So the delete-and-remove-to-trash option needs to be used. How does this work in a marriage? There must be a way to delete and remove the resentment.

The big dilemma is, if both spouses were upset and convinced that they were right, how can they resolve the issue? Are they supposed to lie? Should they each say, "Honey, I was wrong," just so they can have marital harmony? Is this practical?

This system won't bear fruit. It results in the same resentment that the spouse who remained quiet to avoid fights felt, but in this case, both of them feel like the victims.

Your Way Is Not Always the Best Way

THE BEST WAY, IF not the only way, to erase what transpired previously is by viewing things from your spouse's perspective. Once you comprehend why he or she feels like a victim, you can forgive and forget. The focus of the conversation should be, "Please explain to me what made you react this way. Let me understand your perspective."

Also, having the courage and strength to accept that your spouse could be the victim in such a situation, and not you, can be a real challenge, because it confirms that you are at fault. Accepting blame and taking responsibility can be humiliating. It's a direct blow to one's fragile self-image.

Evading culpability is almost a knee-jerk response. If you are shaking your head in disbelief, this is another proof that validates my point. Many of us will go to almost extreme lengths to avoid accepting the blame when anything goes wrong.

Suppose the electric bill was not paid and you are asked, "Why not?" You could probably respond with an excuse like, "The bill didn't come in the mail, I sent the check, they made a mistake, why didn't you remind me earlier, I am overwhelmed, the baby was sick, and more." Or you could say, "I forgot." The problem is, saying "I forgot" is painful. It confirms that I am imperfect and make mistakes, and this affects my self-esteem.

Is there a way to acknowledge the other person's point of view without damaging our own self-esteem?

The key to remember is that, generally, regarding most situations there are no absolutes. There are at least two perspectives. Being at fault is not an absolute; it is only relative. Many times we are both partially at fault. In his world, he is the victim. In her world, she is the victim. That doesn't mean that either one is necessarily right; it's how each of them looks at the situation. Accepting the other's point of view means acknowledging only that in his eyes he is right.

In other words, I have no problem saying, "I'm sorry" about a disagreement, even though I continue to believe that I didn't initiate the particular argument, but rather responded to an attack. If I would have controlled myself and not raised my voice, the fight would not have evolved. So I am also at fault, but not totally.

This thinking keeps one's self-worth intact, while being able to give the other spouse sincere words of regret.

> When dealing with a disagreement, it is important to compromise, to not allow your pride to stand in the way. Many of us feel we will look weak if we take the initiative to reconcile, but doing so is a sign of true strength.[1]

Seeing Things From the Other Side

LET ME GIVE AN example. A husband calls his wife and asks her to pick up the dry cleaning. "I have an important meeting with

---

1. Jacobson, *Toward a Meaningful Life*, p. 53.

the CEO of a large company and I want to wear my favorite suit," he says.

"No problem, it will be my pleasure," she replies.

The husband arrives home and doesn't see his suit. "Honey, did you pick up the suit?"

"Oh my, I forgot," she says. "I can't believe it!"

"You can't believe it? I can't believe it. I called you during the day! How could you have forgotten to do this?"

"I feel so bad," she says.

"Can you explain how you were able to forget something so important to me?" he asks.

"I just got busy and it totally slipped my mind."

"This excuse is unacceptable. If it was important to you, you would have remembered."

"Your accusations are unfounded," she counters. "What you asked for was important to me. I just forgot."

He doesn't let up. "You do what's important to you first and my needs are secondary."

"Enough of your criticism," she says. "I told you I forgot! Stop talking to me this way!"

"Oh, so you're the victim here? First you ignore my request, and now you claim that I am the culprit!"

"Well, how about the day I asked you to pick up my new earrings and you forgot?" she snaps back.

"How dare you compare the two? I work in the office and have to deal with a lot of stress to provide for the family! You're home all day. Surely you can find the time to pick up the dry cleaning!"

"You really think going to the office is more difficult than taking care of the kids, going to the doctor, shopping, paying the bills, buying and preparing dinner, and making sure the laundry is done?" she shoots back.

"Poor girl," he retorts. "You really are overworked...you have no time for anything...you are a full-time servant..."

"Stop it! I hate when you are sarcastic. This is verbal abuse and I won't tolerate it anymore. If you prefer, I will go to work and you can stay home!"

Wow! Look at where a forgotten suit led — to a full-blown fight. Were you able to identify who was right and who was wrong?

I have asked this question to a number of couples, and the majority responded, "It was the wife's fault. She should have remembered to pick up the suit."

What do you think? It's true that the argument began because of her error. But the fight is the fault of both spouses. What do I mean? The wife forgot to pick up the suit. Does her husband think it was intentional? If he does, then their marriage is in trouble, and they have a serious problem. [2]

In a normal, healthy relationship, he would realize that she didn't forget his suit on purpose. She made a mistake. It slipped her mind. Does he ever forget things? Even if he is very organized and never forgets anything, he and his wife do not have to be the same. This wasn't one of the conditions for the marriage. Besides, surely there are other areas where he is not perfect.

If the husband would have accepted that a mistake happened, and he would not have continued to emphasize his frustration, the argument could have ended. But he was relentless. This triggered a defensive response in his wife. No one appreciates being attacked, especially when the omission was unintentional.

So who made the first mistake? The wife.

---

2. The Talmud (*Gittin* 90a) discusses when it is permitted to divorce one's wife. One view is if the wife even burned her husband's stew, this is sufficient reason to divorce her. This sounds somewhat extreme. A woman burns the food and it's time to get divorced? It goes without saying that no rabbi will allow a man to divorce his wife just for this reason. I once heard the following explanation. What our Sages meant was that there is reason to get divorced if she burns *his* food, not *the* food; in other words, if there is malice involved. However, if one spouse simply made a mistake — and that is usually the case — this is not a reason to dissolve a marriage.

Who made the second mistake? The husband.

Who is at fault? Both of them.

By no means am I trying to blame the husband for his reaction. We can all identify with his anger. From a religious perspective, anger should be avoided at all costs. However, we aren't always successful. Since he did not control his anger, he persisted in attacking his wife. At this point, she lost control. If his wife was an angel, she would not have taken his assaults personally. But few people are angels (nor should we expect them to be), and most will not tolerate hearing words that put them down and question their competence.

It's clear that they are dealing with two perspectives; there is room to consider that each person was the one who was wronged. If they step up and admit their responsibility, the couple will be on their way to mending fences.

Imagine that your spouse pushed you. What would be your first reaction? You would probably be shocked, angry, resentful, and frustrated. These are natural, instinctive reactions to provocations.

What if she said, "I'm sorry if I made you angry, but you were stepping on my toe and it really hurt. I was in pain and just reacted."

Once you realize that your spouse's attack was a natural, automatic reaction to something you did, it's much easier to forgive her. This is how we need to see our spouse when we argue. They are not trying to hurt us intentionally; they are simply reacting to being attacked. If both had a chance to think things through, they wouldn't react this way.

We moved to Panama shortly after we married, and I became the rabbi of the Ashkenazi community. My days were consumed with my work at the synagogue, so naturally, when our daughter was born, my wife was her primary caretaker.

One day my wife asked if I could watch the baby. She had to run an errand and assured me that that it would take no more than one hour. Of course I said yes and came home at the scheduled time.

Thank G-d, the hour went by uneventfully. But when the hour passed, my wife didn't show up. This was before everyone had cell phones, so I had no way of contacting her. When another fifteen minutes went by, I started getting anxious. Ten more minutes crawled by, and now I was really upset. She asked me to watch the baby for an hour and look how much time had gone by! Didn't she respect my time?

By then, the baby started crying and acting up, and my stress levels skyrocketed. The baby was surely hungry. Where was her mother? I needed to be in my office, and here I was, at home doing my wife's job.

Fifteen minutes later, she arrived. You can imagine the grand welcome she received.

"Where were you?" I said. "Why didn't you come on time? This is really not fair. What have you been doing for so long?"

I don't remember the reason she gave, but I sure remember the lesson:

"I take care of the baby all day, every day, while you are at the office. If one time you had to share my workload, and I came late, that's okay. Evaluate one hour of your time compared to all the time I spend with the baby."

She was right and I conceded her point immediately. How could I have accosted her for making me spend only forty-five additional minutes watching the baby when she typically did it every day? Besides, why couldn't I give her the benefit of the doubt? She hadn't come home late on purpose.

Some would argue that I was in the right: My wife had committed to be home after one hour and she was very late. It wasn't as if I had nothing else to do; I had important work waiting for me. But seeing her perspective helped me realize that she was *also* right! I had no right to be angry for having to watch the baby for an additional three-quarters of an hour; she did it all day.

Taking the First Step

THE DIFFICULT PART IS, who takes the first step. Who should be the first one to apologize and admit that he is at fault? The second challenge is how to prevent future confrontations.

Every couple needs to work it out. Remember, people don't like to take the first step because they feel this makes them the guilty party, which is an ego crusher. However, we must realize that we are both innocent and guilty. From my perspective I am right. From her vantage point, I am wrong. My self-esteem isn't destroyed when I make the move to fix a fight — I am not saying I am a failure and a loser. I am just saying that I realize I did something that offended her and I am sorry. This is an act of strength, not weakness.

Timing is a critical factor. Admitting that you were at fault will backfire if one or both of you is still angry. There needs to be a cooling-off time, a time-out period. But the situation can't be ignored; it must be resolved at some point. When is a good time? Is it imperative to work things out before retiring for the night? They say that one of the ten commandments of marriage is that the couple should never go to bed without making up. Is this an absolute truth? Would it be so terrible if the couple didn't make up before they went to sleep and waited for the next day?

Practically speaking, if you don't make up before you go to sleep, you won't sleep well. On a more serious note, the longer you wait, the more your unresolved issues will affect your marriage. You had an argument. It happens. Don't let a fight define your marriage — especially if you have a good relationship. Don't let a fight ruin what you have. If you can't tell each other that you are sorry, this shows that you are not able to put your marriage in perspective. The small stuff interferes with the larger picture.

So, yes, it's not a bad idea to put this rule into action: If you fought that day, make sure to say you're sorry before you go to bed for the night.

This doesn't mean you will be able to address the entire issue that you were arguing about before bedtime. That's okay — once you apologize, you have taken a step toward mending your fences. You can decide to find a time to talk about it tomorrow or the next week, this time when you are both calm.

> Never go to bed angry. Better to stay up and fight.

Reconciliation or Reigniting the Argument?

IF YOU CHOOSE TO put off discussing the issue you were fighting about, what do you think will happen when issue arises again?

As long as you are still willing to see your spouse's perspective, you will be able to move past the problem. If you try to prove your point again, the fight will only reignite and worsen.

One of the best pieces of advice I have used personally, and one that I urge newlyweds to adopt, is to hold weekly meetings to discuss issues in your marriage. It is best to discuss issues in a relaxed environment, and the point of the meeting is to find ways to enhance the marriage. Since some couples need to deal with many issues, especially at the onset, it is essential to speak about them in a nonthreatening, nonconfrontational atmosphere. I have found that it is most effective when you go out of your home to discuss these things, maybe over dinner in a restaurant or simply during a walk or drive.

This is also a chance to discuss issues that were the cause of an argument.

When couples sit and talk exclusively about their relationship — what each partner appreciates, what each would like to see changed, and how each can assist the other — they can avoid much unnecessary anguish and hurt.

People sometimes think, *I shouldn't rock the boat*, and choose not to broach a delicate subject. This is counterproductive, because eventually all the issues will surface. When they do, they will feel like a tsunami — appearing without warning and causing devastating harm.

To put it another way, why wait for the person to get sick before providing the necessary vitamins to avoid the ailment?

Keep in mind, however, that there are sensitive situations (such as a fallout with your family members who are getting in the way of the relationship, or childhood traumas that are surfacing) that are so deep rooted that they need to be discussed with a third party, such as a rabbi or a professional. Don't attempt to resolve a situation that is beyond your capabilities.

What happens if you don't set aside time to discuss your issues?

I recall one time, at the beginning of our marriage, my wife said, "And why do you always leave the doors open?"

What is she talking about? I thought. *What doors? My wife must be referring to the front door.* I realized that after I would enter the house, I usually pushed the door to close it. If I pushed too hard it would slam, making an irritating noise. So I pushed gently enough for the door to close without slamming. At times the door would not close completely and remained open. We lived in a three-story apartment building, and we knew our neighbors, so this really didn't concern me.

When my wife accused me of leaving the door open, I thought to myself, *What's the big deal? That occasionally the front door isn't closed? Why is she so annoyed?*

When I mentioned this out loud, she replied, "I'm not talking about the front door. I mean all the doors."

Now I had no clue what she was talking about. "What do you mean? You want me to close the bedroom door?"

"No, I mean all the doors."

"Could you explain?" I asked.

She said, "You have a tendency to open a closet door to remove something and then you leave the door open. So when you take your shoes out of the closet, the door stays open. Or when you get a cup to drink from, the cupboard door is left open."

"You must be hallucinating," I said. "This can't be true." I honestly didn't believe I did this. But I added, "Since I don't notice when I do this, in the future please point it out to me."

Over the next couple of days I learned exactly what she meant. For some inexplicable reason, I had the habit of doing exactly what she had described. It was something that was irritating my wife, but my brain was not registering that I was doing this.

When I realized what I was doing, I began working on it. This bad habit did not disappear easily. I continue to work on it till this day. Believe it or not, I am not "cured," but it's clearly less of a problem than it was before.

What most surprised me was that my wife hadn't mentioned her annoyance at this habit for three years. If we had set aside time to discuss issues earlier in our marriage, I would have been made aware of it sooner.

If you were not successful in avoiding disagreements, all is not lost. You can make up with each other by allowing yourselves to see one another's perspective and apologize. Make sure to set aside time to hash out the issues so they don't lead to further confrontation.

---

21 When a Crisis Strikes

T HE OBJECTIVE OF THIS book is to help people understand the challenges of marriage and provide techniques to improve and enhance the marriage experience. The ideas discussed here are practical and relevant to most relationships. Those who follow these ideas will experience, G-d willing, substantial improvement in all facets of their relationship.

These ideas, however, are meant to help those who are dealing with "regular" issues. At times, though, a crisis happens — an illness in the family, a financial difficulty, a rebellious child, a court case, or some other traumatic event, G-d forbid. At times like these, much effort needs to be invested for these techniques and suggestions to work, simply because everything has become more challenging.[1]

In many instances, a crisis can unite the family. And it should. When faced with a taxing situation that threatens an individual or the family unit, the natural response is to join forces to deal with the situation. However, the strain on the individual

---

1. Of course, if the issue is physical or emotional abuse (G-d forbid), you need to seek professional help as soon as possible.

going through a prolonged test can break his or her spirit and complicates a functioning relationship.

If the problem is short-term, it will probably bring the couple together. When it becomes long-term and it weighs heavily on each spouse, it can take a toll.

When the Pressure Is On

AS WE HAVE DISCUSSED, the reason marriage is so complex is because each person feels his or her ego and self-image is at stake. What my spouse says, with his or her body language and tone of voice, more often than not is translated to, "My intelligence/ goodness/capacity/willingness is being questioned." This normally generates a reaction that can be viewed as both defensive and offensive.

This is true even when there are no external pressures on one's life. Imagine when we are under stress from dealing with a serious concern. The slightest indication that we are being attacked is blown out of proportion and seen as a declaration of war. We become hypersensitive. At these times, the couple needs to work extra hard to avoid criticizing and belittling their partner.

G-d should never test us. But Judaism believes that when He does, He also gives us the stamina and strength to deal with it.

When we are going through a tough time, having faith that we can handle it helps immensely. At the same time, it's important to keep up our spirits and faith. We should do everything in our power to be optimistic and enthusiastic. How is this possible when the situation seems so dark?

This can be achieved when one acknowledges that everything is from G-d and that the purpose of the crisis is to ultimately strengthen the individual and let him prove himself. This is the best attitude to have when going through a trying moment.

We Can Do It

A RELATIVE OF MINE who runs a Chabad house in northern California related the following.

After he finished giving a class, one of the participants approached him and said, "Rabbi, with your concentration level, I'm sure you would be able to crack a plank of wood with your hand."

Every day the woodchopper went into the forest, chopped some wood, and carried the load back to the city to sell. But the woodchopper was getting old. After many years of labor, the job was taking a toll on him and it was getting more and more difficult to carry the load.
One day, in the middle of the winter, he just couldn't manage anymore, so he dropped the load, lifted a hand to heaven, and said, "G-d, relieve me of this burden and take my soul back home."
At that very moment the angel of death appeared. "You called?" he asked.
The man looked at the angel and said, "How nice of you to come! Can you help me lift this load onto my back?"

"I don't believe that's possible," said the rabbi. "I've never done anything like that in my life. But I'm willing to try."

"Rabbi, you can do it; everyone can do it. All you need to do is be convinced that you can be successful and you will be able to accomplish this feat."

He brought a plank of wood and the rabbi attempted to break it, but the first time he tried he almost broke his hand.

"The problem is you were looking at the wood and thinking about how impossible it is to break it with your bare hand, so your hand slowed down at the end. Imagine that the wood doesn't exist and try to get your hand to strike through the plank."

Once again the rabbi got ready, followed the instruction, and then with an "Oo-ha!" he thrust his hand through the plank. Simultaneously, he heard a loud noise — the wood had been broken.

Similarly, if we put our minds to it, we can overcome the difficulties put in our path and achieve the necessary personal and spiritual growth. This can be extremely difficult to accept and it may feel like it's impossible to accomplish, but Judaism affirms that this is true.

Since G-d created the world and has a master plan, it makes sense that when a person is confronted with a problem, it will be one that he or she can manage. Every human being realizes that it's foolish to hire someone for a job that he can't do. Since G-d created the world with a purpose, and He continues to run the world, our difficulties are also part of the plan. And if that's the case, then also built into the plan is our ability to overcome them.

As difficult as it might seem, this idea that we have the potential to overcome all the trials we come across applies to everything we encounter in life.

At a time when Jews were restricted from owning land and working in most businesses, two men whose names were Moshe used to smuggle merchandise from Poland into Russia to sell on the black market. One Moshe was known as Big Moshe since his operation was on a large scale, while the other was known as Small Moshe, because he managed a small business.

One day, Small Moshe was informed that his merchandise had been confiscated. He was ruined. How would he repay all his creditors? It was too much for him and he fainted. Every time he was revived, he asked, "Will I be able to reclaim the goods or recoup my losses?" The answer was always negative, and he'd faint again.

At their wits' end, the family went to ask a blessing from the first Lubavitcher Rebbe, *zy"a*.[2]

---

2. Shneur Zalman of Liadi (1745–1812), founder of the Chabad Chassidic dynasty. Brought the teachings of mysticism to the masses and encouraged Jews to study and be inspired in their service of G-d.

He said, "Tell him the confiscated goods belonged to Big Moshe." When Small Moshe heard this, he recovered his senses.

Soon after, it was confirmed that the contraband really did belong to Big Moshe. The Chassidim asked the Rebbe, "How did you know that the goods belonged to Big Moshe?"

He replied, "Our Sages say that G-d doesn't give people a test they can't manage.[3] I knew that Small Moshe was not in any condition to take such a blow; it was obvious there had been a mix-up because it had to be Big Moshe whose merchandise was lost."

How to Help Your Spouse during a Crisis

THIS BY NO MEANS suggests that if your spouse is recovering from surgery, trauma, or a tragedy, you should just say, "Get over it. Everything is from G-d." This idea is meant to help you get through your own crisis, but when it comes to helping others, especially your spouse, dealing with a trial, your first job is to show empathy: "I can't imagine what you're going through, but I know it's hard. I'm here for you." Later, with care and kindness, you can also offer strength by providing hope and guidance.

The Torah shares with us the details of the moving encounter between Yosef and Binyamin when the two brothers met after twenty-two years of separation.

The verse relates that Yosef cried on Binyamin's neck, and Binyamin cried on Yosef's neck.[4] Rashi explains that each one was crying over the destruction that was to occur in his brother's territory. Yosef was crying over the destruction of the two *Batei Mikdash* (Holy Temples), which would be situated within Binyamin's borders. Binyamin was shedding tears over the

---

3. Midrash, *Bamidbar Rabbah* 21:22.
4. Genesis 45:14.

destruction of the *Mishkan* (Tabernacle) that would be erected in Yosef's land.

The Lubavitcher Rebbe, *zy'a*, asks, "Why didn't the brothers cry over the destruction that was to occur in their own territories?"

He explains that when you experience a problem, you look for how to solve it. You don't cry over it. You seek the source of the pain and see how to deal with it. But when your friend is in pain, the first thing you do is empathize. You don't try to justify another person's pain.[5]

The Mishnah states in *Pirkei Avot*, "Judge people favorably."[6] Once I have judged my friend favorably, all I will have left is to feel for him in his hardship and to share this feeling with him.

The best thing we can do for our spouse who is facing a crisis is show that we are there for them. We are not necessarily going to be able to take away their pain, because we can't really know what they are going through. Once they know you are there for them, and they are ready to hear it, we can encourage them by letting them know that they have the ability to get through their trials.

Be confident that you can overcome all challenges.

5. *Likutei Sichot*, vol. 10, p. 146.
6. *Avot* 1:6.

Conclusion

CHAIM, A BUSINESSMAN, went on a business venture with his right-hand man, Berel. They traveled to a distant country and were very successful. The deal they made generated a fortune. Unfortunately, the boss came down with an aggressive bacterial infection and, without sufficient medical supplies, he was down to his last breaths. He asked for a piece of paper to convey his final words. This is what he wrote:

> To my dear family,
>
> I am saddened that my life has ended early, but I have chosen my confidant Berel to be in charge of my inheritance. I emphatically declare that whatever Berel wants should be distributed to my family. I love you all.
>
> Signed, Chaim Goldstein

Berel was shocked and saddened by the demise of his boss. He arranged for a proper burial and flew back home. During the trip, he thought about his new responsibilities, namely to distribute Chaim's possessions and assets.

He started by dividing the inheritance evenly between the widow and her children. He would keep only 5 percent for himself as payment for his efforts. A short while later, Berel decided that he should be treated equally, because he was such a good and close friend.

As the trip continued, Berel reviewed Chaim's instructions. If Chaim had wanted his family to receive the same amount as himself, then Chaim would have been more specific. *The letter is clear that Chaim wants me to retain all his wealth and manage it for the entire family.*

When Berel arrived home, he went to the family and broke the sad news. After they finished mourning, he produced the note that Chaim had left. It indicated that Berel had complete jurisdiction over the inheritance. "What have you decided?" they asked Berel.

To their dismay, he replied, "I intend to keep everything."

The family was outraged. How could their father do this to them? How could he be so foolish as to entrust all he owned to the manager?

Immediately, they rushed to the rabbi to ask his advice. They presented him with all the facts and poured out their anxieties and frustrations. The rabbi listened and was at a loss as to what to do. It seemed like there was no way out. For a reason unknown to him, the father had given over his assets to Berel, and now Berel had the option to keep it all.

The rabbi said, "Call me tomorrow and we will talk again." The rabbi knew that there had to be a catch. Chaim was a wise man and very dedicated to his family. He wouldn't have made such a foolish miscalculation and put all his trust in his manager.

> Two old friends met after many years. "How are you doing?" Leah asked.
> Myrna: "All is well. Did you hear that I got married?"
> Leah: "No, how nice. How is your husband?"
> Myrna: "He is an angel."
> Leah: "You're really lucky. Mine is still alive."

The next morning the rabbi summoned Chaim's family and Berel to his office. He asked to see the original note and read it carefully. "My dear friends," the rabbi said, "the note clearly states that 'whatever Berel wants should be distributed to my family.'"

"Berel, what do you want?" the rabbi asked.

"I want to keep everything, all the money we made abroad and all the assets that Chaim owned."

The family was expecting the worst, and now it seemed that their fears were about to come true.

Looking at both parties, the rabbi stated, "I rule that the deceased's family gets everything."

"How can this be?" Berel shouted. "This is against the law! It says explicitly that the assets should be distributed as I want."

"I am following the note exactly," the rabbi insisted, "It says, whatever you want should be given to the family. YOU WANTED IT ALL, SO THAT'S EXACTLY WHAT THE FAMILY GETS!"

Berel finally realized his greed in wanting to keep the entire inheritance. Acknowledging the genius of the rabbi, he left disappointed. At last the family understood how clever their father had been. He knew that Berel could deny making money on the trip, so he devised a plan to test the honesty and loyalty of his manager.

This is a wonderful message for marriage: *Whatever you want, give to your spouse.*

What do we all want? To be respected, appreciated, complimented, loved, understood, accepted, pleased… so do the same for your spouse.

We have discussed different techniques and ideas to enhance and improve a marriage. Let's summarize these ideas:

⊕ Recognize your differences.
⊕ See your partner's point of view.
⊕ Don't take things personally.
⊕ Find activities you can do together.
⊕ Become good friends, not just marriage partners.
⊕ Focus on what you can do for your spouse.
⊕ Don't make calculations about who sacrifices more.
⊕ Look at life from your spouse's perspective.
⊕ Avoid being egocentric; be humble and flexible.
⊕ Look only at the positive aspects of your spouse.

- Make your spouse feel that he or she is your priority.
- Don't take your spouse for granted.
- Make an effort — good things don't happen by themselves.
- Convey your needs to your spouse in a clear way.
- Every wife should have a hobby that increases her self-esteem.
- Make time weekly to talk about your marriage and how to improve it.
- Remember that it's part of your G-dly mission to achieve marital harmony.
- Treat her like a queen and him like a king.
- Give more positive feedback, less negative feedback.
- Shower your spouse with compliments.
- Remember your commitment to a long-term marriage.
- Try to work on unconditional love.
- Steer away from the part of your spouse's personality that you don't appreciate.
- Accept your spouse as he or she is.
- Understand your differences because of the country, community, and family you come from and work on resolving them.
- Try to keep your parents from interfering in your marriage.
- Avoid criticism and anger at all costs.
- Work as a team.
- Refrain from speaking in a way that is threatening to your spouse.
- If an argument starts, take a break and postpone the conversation until you are both calmer.
- Don't sweep arguments under the rug. Resolve them.
- When necessary, seek professional assistance.

Before I conclude, I want to discuss this last piece of advice for a moment. Sometimes you need professional help or even a friend to help you communicate with your spouse. If your marriage is in gridlock, a third party can get you both moving and focused on solutions.

Why does it help to have another person involved? It's much easier to communicate via e-mail or messenger rather than face-to-face. You are less vulnerable and therefore won't get into a fight so easily. This is why marital therapy can be so effective. When we are trying to resolve a problem alone, we are so busy trying to win the discussion that we can't hear the other person's points. When we are talking to a therapist, we can listen more attentively. Unfortunately, in the first sessions each side is usually trying to convince the therapist that they are right, so it's hard to progress. But if we come to therapy with the correct approach — to learn what we can do differently and what we're doing wrong — the marriage will usually improve.

The saying goes, "If you think education is expensive, just try the alternative (ignorance)." Making a marriage work and thrive requires great effort, but it's definitely worth it — and the alternative (divorce) is far worse.

As parents, we will do anything for the well-being of our children. There is no greater gift to them than to maintain a harmonious marital relationship.

When we generate peace in our home, then we can hope to see harmony in our community and eventually peace in the entire world.

Make sure to do things for your spouse.

Appendices

The Dating Game

T HE MARRIAGE PROCESS BEGINS when two people meet, start to date, and feel chemistry for each other. Over time their relationship blossoms until they come to feel the excitement of having found their *bashert* (soul-mate). At some point, they take the next step and become engaged, convinced that their marriage will last and be mutually fulfilling.

Yet a large number of couples end up divorcing. What happened to the love they once had for each other? In some cases, these couples were together

> Love is a beautiful dream. Marriage is the alarm clock.

for months or even years before they married. How can two people stay together happily in an extended courtship and then divorce after a short marriage?

Not Who You Thought They Were

I ONCE HEARD A rabbi explain the biblical story of the Jewish patriarch Yaakov and his wives, Leah and Rachel. As you may recall, Yaakov worked seven years for his future father-in-law in order to marry his beloved Rachel. Finally the wedding took place, only for Yaakov to discover the next morning that he had wed Leah and not the Rachel of his dreams!

The rabbi said, "This happens to all married people. You think you are marrying one person, but then you discover that the person you ended up with is not who you thought."

Before the wedding, the future bride and groom feel that an eternal bond exists between them. They can't imagine ever doing anything that will break that bond irreparably. When they marry, and the ring is placed on the bride's finger, the emotional bond that they feel is solidified. You might imagine that marriage would only strengthen their bond and that they should be able to face any challenge together without it impacting negatively on their relationship.

Yet often the opposite occurs.

The reason is simple. As long as the groom is aware that his connection with his bride can end easily, he will make an extra effort to please her, fearing that if he drops the ball she will leave him. Obviously the same is true of the bride. Once they marry, they know that the relationship will not terminate over a petty argument, so why give in? There is no need to invest the same amount of energy into the relationship as they did before they married. The ring is already on her finger! So in their minds, they think, *Finally it's his/her turn to take the initiative. In the past, I went out of my way to apologize even though I knew I was right, but this can't go on forever. In all fairness, when (in my opinion) my spouse is at fault, let him/her apologize!*

Meanwhile, the other spouse feels, *Wow, this relationship has taken a sudden turn. Until now, he/she was able to admit a mistake was made. Now he doesn't think that he can do any wrong.*

This paradigm shift is common among married couples. Now that they are married, they don't feel the need to change and admit their mistakes. Why should they? After all, what is the other spouse going to do about it now?

More than one wife has asked her husband, "Why is it that before we got married, you always gave me flowers, a card, a gift, but lately I've gotten nothing?"

"Are you kidding?" he replied. "That was the sales pitch!"

When marriage partners are not willing to make the effort for their marriage, they begin to feel that the person they married is not who they thought they were, and the relationship deteriorates.[7]

> If men would treat their wives like they treat their fiancées, there would be fewer divorces and more bankruptcies.

The Ties That Bind

IT SEEMS THAT WHAT creates the initial connection between the couple during their courtship is not necessarily what's essential for maintaining a commitment over the long term.

When a couple dates, they are looking for their Mr. or Mrs. Right — their Romeo or Juliet. For a woman, Romeo is someone who will give her emotional, financial, and physical security — a strong, capable and determined person who will be kind to her. Meanwhile, Romeo is primarily looking for a Juliet who will fill his physical needs.

After the wedding, Juliet needs affirmation that she is the priority in Romeo's life, usually in the form of compliments and attention. Their physical attraction is most often not sufficient to nurture her self-esteem over time. She craves the words, gifts, and tenderness that prove she is beloved and special. When this doesn't happen, and her strong and determined Romeo has become more demanding of her and more focused on himself, the illusion that Romeo will continue to make her feel special starts to vanish. She begins to feel stressed and unhappy.

---

7. See Chapter 11, "Make It Work, Make the Effort."

Romeo, on the other hand, who wanted a sweet, soft-spoken, caring, and sensitive Juliet, now expects his wife to be able to fend for herself. She must be able to run his household, though this may require that she be tough with the domestic help, that she be able to stand her ground when it comes to getting a better price, and be mainly responsible for raising the children (and in some cases also contributing to the income), while still looking beautiful and fulfilling his needs. This, of course, is not realistic, so he begins to reject her.

What's happening here?

The initial attraction that a couple feels for each other often ends up becoming the source of their problems in the marriage. She liked the fact that he was tough; this gave her a sense of security. Now she despises that fact that he is opinionated. He liked her sweet and soft personality. Now he sees her as too soft because she allows others to manipulate her. Certainly attraction is important, but one needs to choose a spouse not just by external features. A life decision should not be made just because the man makes the woman feel good, or just because the woman makes the man look good.

In order for a relationship to flourish over time, both partners need to be aligned on four levels:

⊕ Physical;
⊕ Emotional;
⊕ Rational;
⊕ Spiritual.

In other words, each individual should be asking these questions:

Physical: Am I physically attracted to this person? Do I find the person's appearance appealing?

Emotional: Do I feel emotionally attached to this person? Is there any chemistry between us? Do I enjoy this person's company? Do I feel comfortable in the person's presence?

Rational: This refers to things that are important for maintaining a long-term relationship. Is he or she kind, friendly, compassionate? How is this person's relationship with his or her mother, brother, uncle, and friends? Does the person have his or her ego in check? What do this person's coworkers feel about him or her? Is the individual a hard worker or lazy? Are material gains my prospective spouse's entire focus? How do our family values compare?

Spiritual: Do we share the same religion? Is our level of commitment to observance similar? Are we on the same spiritual-growth path?

Most people who are dating have a list that enumerates all the qualities they are looking for in a spouse, whether they've actually written it down or it is in their minds. Take a look at your list. Chances are, everything on your list falls into one of those four categories. Now ask yourself: Of these four categories, which one do I think is critical for me to clinch the deal and marry my prospective spouse?

You will most probably answer: the emotional. If a person has no feeling at all for the other person, then probably they won't end up getting married.

In the non-religious world, it goes without saying that men are primarily focused on the physical component. They evaluate the physical appearance of a potential wife. Women too want their spouse to be handsome and good-looking. Yet the emotional connection is still primary. If there is no emotional connection at all, the relationship will falter.

So, before the wedding, both parties are usually concerned with the emotional and physical aspects of their relationship. They don't pay that much attention to the rational and spiritual dimensions. Even if one of them senses that their marriage will be a challenge, either because they don't share the same religious outlook, or one or both of them don't really get along with people, it's difficult to terminate the relationship once the emotions are engaged. As the saying goes, "Love is blind." If everything looks good on the outside and it feels right, they will find reasons to say that everything will work out.

After marriage, however, the spiritual and rational aspects kick in, and over time, these factors become increasingly important. If a couple has no compatibility in these areas, the courtship may have been successful, but the marriage will not last.

Take Off the Blinders

MANY DIVORCES COULD BE avoided if people don't fall into this trap. For this reason, it's ideal to get as much information about the other person as you can before you let yourself get emotionally involved. If your brain tells you that this relationship will fail (probably because the person is lacking in the rational and spiritual categories), don't let your heart persuade you to move ahead.

Perhaps this explains why many cultures have developed courtship customs to avoid getting carried away by the emotional and physical aspects of a relationship. On one extreme, a couple's marriage might be prearranged by the parents without the children's involvement. On the other extreme, some people date for many years before deciding to marry.

In my Chassidic tradition, couples meet several times and spend a number of hours conversing about their values, experiences, and lives. If each feels confident that the other person would be an appropriate partner, they become engaged. However, they meet only after they have looked into each other's backgrounds to make sure that they are of good character. Only after they are sure that the individual is the kind of person they would like to marry do they meet and see if they are compatible in other areas. First the focus is on the spiritual and rational aspects, before the emotional or physical component is considered.

Some people have a hard time understanding this type of

dating. How can a couple see each other for such a short period of time and make such an important decision? Can one really get to know a person in only twenty hours? Is this even a responsible thing to do? After all, we are talking about a long-term relationship that will eventually involve children.

Logically, they think, a couple who has known each other for twelve months or more should have a greater marriage success rate than a couple who has known each for only a short period of time. According to statistics, however, extended courtship periods do not necessarily lead to longer-lasting marriages and fewer divorces. In fact, marriages in religious communities, where the couples date for just a few weeks, last longer than those in secular communities.

This by no means suggests that all religious people have great marriages. Every married couple experiences challenging and difficult times. This is inevitable and normal, and sometimes a marriage suffers when this happens, no matter how religious the couple is. But in the long run, the more religiously observant the couple is, the better their chances at staying married.

Why is this so?

One reason is connected to the four categories I mentioned above. For a marriage to last, a couple needs to have a strong spiritual and rational foundation. This is what religious people try to discover before looking at the physical and emotional aspects. For this reason, the research that occurs prior to the couple's meeting is crucial. What type of person is he or she? What do people have to say about this person? What is the person's track record? Do we share the same values? Do we believe in having large families? Are we going to educate our children in the same religious values? What type of family is the person from?

This way, issues that may arise after marriage and might be a matter of contention are generally addressed in the research stage, before the courting process even begins.

To the men reading this book, I would say, when you see a

cool sports car, you would probably get all the stats from the seller before you buy it. Ignoring these fundamentals in favor of a shiny paint job would be foolish.

I would ask the women reading this book: Would most men you know butter up a retailer if they thought that by doing so they could get an especially reduced price? Chances are, they would. Most men will say anything to make a woman feel loved when they want to be in a relationship; this does not necessarily mean they are making a commitment that is engraved in stone. In other words, let the buyer (prospective bride) beware.

I strongly urge dating couples to make a list of desirable traits and qualities they are looking for in a spouse and assign points to each quality and characteristic. Then rate your potential marriage partner and honestly evaluate the chances of future success.

For example, you might write that you are looking for a husband who is:

- ⊕ responsible
- ⊕ hardworking
- ⊕ intelligent
- ⊕ goodhearted
- ⊕ educated (with a BA at least)
- ⊕ sociable and well-liked
- ⊕ strong
- ⊕ handsome
- ⊕ respectful
- ⊕ humble

and who:

- ⊕ likes to read
- ⊕ enjoys adventure
- ⊕ eats healthfully
- ⊕ exercises regularly

- has a good sense of humor
- loves kids
- doesn't smoke, drink, or do drugs

If you are a man, you might be looking for a wife who is:

- caring
- giving
- loving
- smart
- from a good family
- outgoing (or quiet)
- friendly
- organized
- career-oriented
- interested in having a large family
- understanding
- good-looking
- good at running a household
- interested in travel
- not a big spender
- not arrogant

Take this list and divide these characteristics into three categories:

(1) Essential
(2) Important
(3) Would be nice

It might be *essential* for the prospective husband not to drink or do drugs, it's *important* that he eat healthfully, and it *would be nice* if he likes adventure. The man looking for a prospective wife might find it *essential* that she not be arrogant, *important* that she be good-looking, and it *would be nice* if she is interested in travel.

When you meet a prospect for marriage, you can evaluate if the match is worth pursuing according to the things you feel are essential for you. This prevents you from getting involved emotionally and ending up with pain and regret if the person was not really the right one for you.

> The matchmaker asked the young man, "So what are you looking for in your future wife?"
>
> "She should be a nice person, from a good family, with a large dowry, quite intelligent, attractive, and dedicated to family values."
>
> "Whew! With all those requirements, I can marry off six people."

When you are looking into a prospective spouse's background, a person who has been divorced a number of times should raise a red flag. Maybe the relationship will work, but try to find out more: Why did the person get divorced? Is he/she a difficult person or is he/she just bad at choosing the right marriage partner? Filing for bankruptcy a couple of times, or having no friends, are other warning signs.

Once the couple has obtained the pertinent information, they can examine the emotional and physical aspects of the relationship. Now they can ask: Do I like how this person looks? Can I have a decent conversation with him or her? Is there a spark between us?

These questions do not take that much time to evaluate. Deciding whether you like the appearance of the other person is not rocket science. To judge your rapport and the flow of the conversation is relatively easy.

The point is, marriage is not just an emotional decision; it also needs to be an intellectual one. Admittedly, it can be quite difficult to make the decision by first thinking it through rationally — it's much easier to let your emotions take control — but it's worth it in the long run so that you avoid the heartache of a divorce.

Needless to say, any agreements you made with your prospective spouse should stand after marriage. If both of you have decided to live in a certain type of community based on your mutual religious level and needs, then it's not okay for one party to suddenly decide that they must live among a different society. If they do decide to make a lifestyle change after marriage, it should be mutual and well thought-out.

Most people would consider this to be stating the obvious, but for many people it isn't so obvious. A newlywed couple I knew had a serious disagreement. The wife claimed that prior to their wedding, they had agreed to several conditions, and now the groom wanted to renegotiate.

When I approached the groom's family, hoping to clear up what I thought was a misunderstanding, I was surprised to hear that in their minds, agreements that are made before marriage are not binding. I had a difficult time digesting their point. However, they insisted that this was common knowledge, and this was the way things were done in their family.

"Well, the woman's family has different customs," I said to them. "A commitment made before the marriage is fundamental and nonnegotiable."

A father on his deathbed summoned his son and said, "I need to share with you the two most important secrets of business."

"Yes, Father, tell me," the boy said eagerly.

"If you promise to deliver merchandise by a certain day, you must always keep your word," the father whispered with his fading strength.

"Father, what is the second one?" the son asked urgently.

With his last breath, the father croaked, "Never promise."

Trust is the basis of any relationship. If you say it, obey it. Yes, it can happen that, over the years, partners evolve and interests and hobbies shift, and the couple needs to reevaluate decisions they made when they were first married. But this should not happen during the first years of marriage, and any major life changes they make should be discussed.

Bottom line, before a couple decides to marry, it's important for them to establish that not only do they like each other and are physically attracted to each other, but that they also have mutual interests and religious values.

What About Love?

IS LOVE A COMPONENT of this decision?

Definitely, but not love as understood by modern society. There needs to be a feeling of connection, but not necessarily the head over heels type of love people seek nowadays.[8]

Isn't getting married before falling in love a little risky?

Let me answer that question with another one: Is true love a component in a secular marriage?

Did you answer yes? But think about it: Is it love or is it infatuation?

The reality is, all courtships are fragile, and if one disagreement is all it takes to end the relationship, then what they have for each other is not true love. It might feel as passionate and strong as love, but it isn't; it's a façade, a fake feeling of love. Let us not confuse the two.[9]

We generally marry someone we presume will give us something: security, love, care, a nice life. But that kind of relationship

---

8. See Chapter 8, "Love Is Not an Accident."
9. Ibid.

is conditional: As long as the other person is giving me those things, I will love him back. But the love we have for our spouse needs to evolve into true love — unconditional love that is not based on externals. For that we need to make an effort: before the marriage, we check out the person to ensure that his or her values and character align with ours; after marriage, we work hard to give the other person his or her needs.

Can a person find out everything about his potential partner prior to marriage? Of course not. Even people who date for a long time don't find out everything there is to know about the other person. And often, they are blinded by attraction, or they haven't confronted the types of issues that come up once the couple has formalized their relationship.

The religious couple, by contrast, understands that they will need to work on their marriage once the wedding is over. They enter the marriage with eyes open, knowing that it will not all be smooth sailing, but they are ready to support each other when difficulties arise.

> A woman sat next to a man on an airplane and casually mentioned, "You look like my third husband."
>
> "How many times have you been married?" the gentleman asked politely.
>
> She looked at him pointedly and answered, "Twice."

The decision to marry should not be solely an emotional one. One should make sure that a potential spouse has desirable character traits and similar values.

Male-Female Roles in Judaism

A RE YOU A TRADITIONALIST? Do you believe the man earns the money and the woman raises the children? Or do you advocate equal roles — both of you earn the money and you share household responsibilities? Or maybe the husband should be a stay-at-home dad while the wife gets the power job?

The question of male and female roles can be a source of great conflict in a marriage. Traditionally, the man is the head of the household. He is responsible for providing for the family, while the woman runs the home. Today, these roles are sometimes different. In many homes, the woman works as well, or the man spends his days studying Torah, while the woman supports the family completely. In some families, the roles are even completely reversed if the wife has the better-paying job and it makes more sense for her husband to stay home and take care of the family.

Even if the couple has agreed to an arrangement, whether explicitly or tacitly, this can still be a source of conflict. Perhaps the wife thought she would enjoy working out of the home, but when she started having children, she realized that she wants to be home. Maybe the husband always envisioned a stay-at-home wife, and she couldn't imagine not working. Maybe the man has lost his job (an all too common occurrence nowadays), and the couple realizes they could do better if the woman gets a job.

Much of the conflict arises because one or both spouses are confused by exactly what their roles and obligations in the relationship should be. Even if they decide to have a different arrangement, it's important to be aware that they have chosen — hopefully mutually — to do something different than what is expected. This way, if circumstances change, they will be better able to make decisions without conflict.

A couple came to me in a mess. They were fighting a lot and one of the major issues of contention was who should be taking care of the baby.

The husband said, "I go out to work and provide for my family. My wife should be responsible for taking care of the baby."

"I can't do it all by myself," she responded. "I need a breather sometimes. I'm happy to take care of the baby, but I'd like it if you could take over even for twenty minutes when you get home. That will give me a much needed break."

> "How can you be married for so many years without ever fighting?" Ben asked Michael. "When we got married we made an agreement: I make all the major decisions, and my wife makes all the minor ones. It's been forty years and I haven't had one decision to make yet."

It took the husband a while to realize that it was okay for him to take over responsibility for his baby for a little while. It didn't mean she was neglecting her responsibilities, but she needed some time for herself, too.

Men's and Women's Roles in the Torah

The story is told of a rookie insurance salesman who heard screaming when he approached a house to make his next sale. It was clear that the couple were in middle of a "world war."

Should I ring the bell or come back? he asked himself.

He decided to ring the bell.

Lo and behold, as soon as the bell rang, the screaming stopped. A minute later a man opened the door and said, "How can I help you?"

"Excuse me, sir," the salesman said. "I sell insurance. I'd like to talk to the person in charge."

"Please come back in about half an hour," the man replied, "because we are in the middle of discussing that very question."

The Torah defines the marriage relationship as one in which the man naturally leads. It states, "The man shall dominate his wife."[1] Our Sages also say, "Who is a proper woman? One who fulfills her husband's will."[2] Furthermore, the Rambam writes, "A wife should treat her husband the way someone treats a king — never seek to do him any harm."[3]

Jewish law dictates that when parents simultaneously order a child to do contradictory things, he should listen to his father, because his mother is also required to obey her husband. This is also why the Torah commands, "A man should fear his mother and his father."[4] Rashi explains that this statement (which is

---

1. Genesis 3:16.
2. *Tanna D'Vei Eliyahu Rabbah*, ch. 9.
3. *Hilchot Ishut*, ch. 15.
4. Leviticus 19:3.

addressed only to men) tells us that a married woman's priority is her husband, not her parents.[5]

It seems crystal clear that the Jewish view is that the man is the head of the household. As we will see, this in no way diminishes the significance of the woman's role.

If the Torah views the man as more dominant in the household, why should we accept the outside world's opinion on the role and rights of women in marriage?

Let us begin with a simple example. According to biblical law,[6] a man may marry more than one wife. This law doesn't seem to be a very helpful way to teach men about relationships. Neither is this a good tool to build a woman's self-worth and image. On the contrary, as we mentioned in Chapter 11, "Make It Work, Make the Effort," a man who expects his wife to give him everything he needs, but doesn't make the effort to provide for her needs, is not boosting her self-esteem, to say the least.

So how can the Torah sanction polygamy if it can be detrimental to a marriage? In fact, it's difficult to fathom how a person who marries more than one wife can have a deep relationship with any of his spouses. For such a man, marriage becomes an ego trip, a way to get personal satisfaction without the need to work on himself. If you are married to only one person, you have to work on your ego to permit the other person's needs to merge with yours, or you won't have a marriage.

By the way, Jewish law no longer allows a man to marry several women.[6] Although we find that in the Torah polygamy was permitted, it was not necessarily encouraged. It opened my eyes to consider that none of our patriarchs took a second wife of his own volition. Avraham was childless, so his wife, Sarah,

---

5. Rashi, Leviticus 19:3.

6. *Shulchan Aruch, Even HaEzer* 1:9.

suggested that Avraham marry her maidservant. And although Yitzchak, too, was childless, he did not use this option. Yaakov, who ended up with four wives, intended to marry only one, Rachel. Neither Yosef nor Moshe married more than one wife. It seems that the Torah law that allows polygamy is connected to procreation out of necessity rather than personal pleasure.

In addition, just because the man is considered dominant and his wife should "respect him as she would respect a king," this does not mean that the man may ignore his wife. On the contrary, the man must cherish his wife and do whatever he can to please her. The Torah commands men to go all out to please their spouse from the onset of their marriage. The Torah says clearly, "He shall make his wife happy."[7] In the words of the Rambam, "he should love her more than he loves himself."

But how do we reconcile these two ideas: "I am in charge, but I need to please my wife"?

The Importance of Hierarchy

WHY DID G-D ASSIGN these roles to men and women? Why should one get to be the king in the home? Why can't both of them be able to fill the same roles?

Consider the structure of a big corporation. Each employee — from vice president to secretary — has a specific role in the company. And at the top is the CEO who runs the whole show. Does this mean that the vice president or, for that matter, the secretaries need to feel intimidated and controlled? Of course not. It means that after employees have given their opinion about a matter that arises in the company, the final decision belongs to the CEO.

---

7. Deuteronomy 24:5.

Rashi comments, "Two kings cannot simultaneously wear the same crown."[8] For a family to be healthy and functional, it's important that there is a hierarchy, a chain of command. This by no means suggests that the husband should manage his marriage like a tyrant. He should always and foremost act like a mensch. In some cases, he can and should give in to his wife. At other times, he may expect to have things done his way. The main thing is that he take into account the interests and needs of his family in any decision.

Whenever I put up mezuzot in the home of a family, I generally share with them a fascinating idea about this mitzvah.

Why is the mezuzah placed on a slant? According to one opinion, it should be positioned vertically. Another opinion believes it should be placed horizontally. The Jewish law is to recognize both opinions. For this reason, we position the mezuzah in an inclined manner as a compromise.

The message is very powerful. We must always look to compromise, even when we have different opinions and perspectives.

What should a woman do when she disagrees with her husband? Should she always verbally consent to his will? Let us look for an answer in the Torah. Did the matriarchs follow this pattern?

Did Sarah always agree with Avraham? No. She argued that Ishmael had to be expelled from their home, and G-d Himself seconded her motion.[9] How about Rivka? Clearly not. Her husband, Yitzchak, wanted to give the blessings to Eisav. Rivka knew he did not deserve it, so she arranged for their younger son, Yaakov, to get her husband's blessing.[10]

Let's talk about Rachel. On the surface, she showed disloyalty to Yaakov, her husband-to-be, by allowing her sister, Leah, to join

---

8. See Rashi on Genesis 1:16.

9. Genesis 21:12.

10. Ibid. 27:8–13.

Yaakov under the marriage canopy in her stead. But her only desire was to protect her sister's reputation — not to rebel against Yaakov.[11]

Based on this, we can better understand the Lubavitcher Rebbe's explanation of the saying, "Who is a proper woman — she who 'makes' her husband's will."[12] The Hebrew word *osah* can be understood as both "fulfills" or "makes" his will.[13] Sarah "made" Avraham's will. Rivka "made" Yitzchak's will: Once he learned that he blessed Yaakov rather than Eisav, he affirmed Yaakov's blessing. The point is, sometimes our matriarchs fulfilled their husbands' will, and sometimes they had the insight to do the right thing even though it was in opposition to their husbands' will. Later their spouses accepted their decision; the matriarchs had "made" their husbands' will.

Along these lines, the Talmud[14] discusses the difference between Korach's wife and On ben Peles's wife. The former instigated him to rebel against Moshe; the latter prevented her husband from getting involved. Korach died because he followed his wife's advice. On ben Peles survived in the merit of his wife.[15]

Bottom line, every woman needs to realize that her husband is above her in the family pyramid. But the husband needs to remember that G-d is above both of them, and that G-d expects him to treat his wife with dignity and respect — and to be open to heeding her advice since she may have an insight into a situation that he is missing.

---

11. Rashi, Genesis 29:25.

12. *Hilchot Ishut*, ch. 15.

13. Perhaps we can add another interpretation. The word for "her husband" is *baalah*, which literally means "her master." *Ishah*, "woman," symbolizes the Jewish people. In that sense, the saying could be read, "Who is a proper Jew? One who fulfills her Master's [i.e., G-d's] will."

14. *Sanhedrin* 110a.

15. Talmud, *Sanhedrin* 109b, 110a.

Judaism does not encourage the husband to control his wife with an iron fist. True, she should respect him, but as the Rambam wrote, "He must love her more than he loves himself."[16] If you love someone more than you love yourself, that person will never feel manipulated, controlled, or intimidated.

A man once came into my office quite upset and said, "Rabbi, my wife traveled to Colombia and went shopping without me. Don't I have the right to get a full accounting of exactly what she bought and how much she spent?"

"Definitely, you have the right," I said. "But if you feel compelled to exercise this right, your marriage is in big trouble."

In this case, this man had a need to control his wife and didn't trust her. I wanted him to know that if he kept going along this track, he was endangering his marriage.

If you want a long-lasting marriage, don't get caught up in "he should, she should." Each of you has an important role in your marriage, and neither role is any less significant than the other. Even if you decide to split your tasks differently than in a traditional marriage, you should still have in mind that the man is respected as a king and the woman is cherished and loved as his queen.

Like the lesson of the mezuzah, a marriage requires compromise to function. When we live in peace and harmony, we invite G-d's blessings into our home. We can achieve that only through giving and humility.

> In Judaism, the man is the head of the household. He gets the final say, but a wise man will listen to his wife and respect her insights. He must cherish her and make sure all her needs are met, and she must respect him and fulfill his needs:
> a formula for a long-lasting, healthy marriage.

---

16. *Hilchot Ishut*, ch. 15.

The Physical Connection

THE TALMUD STATES THAT men are more interested in physical intimacy than women.[1] You probably didn't need the Talmud to tell you that. The question is, how do you balance the desire for intimacy with the recognition that the union is in essence a spiritual one in which two souls merge as one?

The Talmud[2] relates that the Rabbis once asked G-d to remove the desire for physical relations to curtail the evil inclination. The results were not what they expected. According to the Talmud, "the hens stopped laying eggs, the cows stopped having calves, and humans stopped having children." Realizing the reason for this phenomenon, the Rabbis prayed again. Only this time, they asked G-d just to "blind the evil urge in one eye" — that is, to reduce its power over man.

For a marriage to last, the couple needs effective communication, common interests, similar values, few arguments, and a flexible outlook, so each spouse can see the other's point of view. For a marriage to thrive, the couple must experience physically and emotionally satisfying intimacy.

---

1. *Ketubot* 64b.
2. *Yoma* 69a.

A woman came to see me and told me her marriage was on the brink of collapsing. "What's the problem?" I asked. "Do you fight a lot?"

"Not at all," she said.

"Does he support the family?"

"Yes, he makes a decent living."

"Is he faithful to the marriage?" I asked.

"I believe so," she replied.

"Okay, I give up. What are the issues?"

"Well, we rarely have marital relations."

"Why is that?" I asked.

"He says that I am overweight," she mumbled.

"What have you done about this?" I wanted to know.

"Nothing. I feel so depressed and rejected that I've had no interest in spending time with him."

The husband wasn't feeling attracted to his wife, and the wife was feeling rejected by her husband. I wasn't surprised that they were having trouble in this area.

"Do you want to save your marriage?" I asked the wife.

"Yes, of course," she responded.

"You will need to put in some effort," I said. "Are you willing?" I asked. Then I added the punch line, "Make an effort to go on a serious diet, and everything will work out."

She followed my advice and the results were positive. The marriage improved and their family grew.

Like everything else in a marriage relationship, women and men view this aspect of marriage differently. And that can become a source of contention that can break a marriage. Often, although a couple may argue about various issues, the underlying problem is dissatisfaction in this area, especially for the man. Understanding the other's perspective of physical intimacy can make the difference between a happy, fulfilling marriage and one where both parties are dissatisfied, leading to fights and resentment.

The P's vs. the A's

FOR A WOMAN, PHYSICAL intimacy will function if everything else is working well. For a husband, everything will function if physical intimacy is working well. As we've said throughout this book, the third P stands for "Pleasure." For the male psyche, the pleasure derived from intimacy is mainly what keeps him interested in the relationship. It's self-understood that women also derive pleasure from marital relations, but this is secondary to their primary need to feel cared for and loved — their need for Affection.

> A simple *melamed* (teacher) who taught children in a distant village would come home once a year for the holidays to be with his family. After many years, he was finally offered a job in the village where he lived, so he was delighted. After a couple of weeks, the rabbi summoned him to his office. "Moishe," said the rabbi, "your wife is complaining that you don't have marital relations." "Rabbi, when I worked in the other shtetl I would come home once a year, and each year we would have a child. I can't afford to have children every month."

I once heard a psychologist say, "Intimacy doesn't make the marriage; it's a way to celebrate a successful marriage." But many people would disagree. They are convinced that it is precisely the intimacy that builds the marriage. This seems to reflect the different perspectives of men and women. Men think that it's the intimacy that makes the marriage. For women, intimacy can function only as a way to celebrate a functioning relationship.

This poses a problem.

Pursuing pleasure for its own sake is a totally selfish pursuit. Its goal is gratifying a corporeal desire. It's all about personal satisfaction. In marriage, this is both harmful and damaging. As long as the individual is just looking out for his or her personal contentment, the spouse will feel neglected and abandoned. The reason is that the wife truly needs to spend private time with her husband outside the bedroom. But if he is looking only for physical intimacy, he will surely end up ignoring her needs.

> A husband that focuses on his own physical gratification doesn't provide his wife with any of the emotional and spiritual gratification that is the basis of her vitality.[3]

Men need to make a point of focusing on the woman's need for emotional support and not just on their own pursuit of pleasure. It is worthwhile to note that the better the emotional bond, the more fulfilling the physical union. Therefore, the husband should be very focused on satisfying his wife's cravings and needs. This creates a "win/win" situation for both parties.

This is why one of the three biblical obligations a husband has to provide his wife is marital relations.[4] It seems that it should be the opposite, since it is the husband who seems to need physical intimacy in the relationship more than the woman. However, by placing this obligation on the man, it helps him remember the emotional and spiritual aspect of their connection and, hopefully, brings him to focus on her needs. This is why the emphasis of the mitzvah is on what he needs to do for her and not vice versa.

Once, I was visited by a woman who was quite depressed. The cause of her anxiety was her marriage relations. She told me that her husband was an excellent provider, but when it came to marital relations, he expected to be attended to as if they had a one-way relationship.

---

3. Arush, *The Garden of Peace*, p. 134.

4. Exodus 21:9 and Rashi there.

GPS FOR A HAPPIER MARRIAGE

This husband had never learned anything about the husband's obligations and responsibilities with regard to intimacy, so he thought that it was all about his gratification. He felt he did his part in providing for his wife and that their physical relations were for him alone.

According to the Torah, a man is obligated to provide his wife's basic needs: food, clothing, shelter — and marital relations. This is the man's responsibility to his wife. The *Shulchan Aruch* states, "If a man perceives that his wife is interested and looking for closeness, he should attend to her."[5]

Similarly, Rabbi Yaakov Emden writes[6] that "one should converse with his spouse before becoming intimate, and after intimacy, one should not retreat quickly lest his spouse feel that the act was done out of sheer personal gratification, without sensitivity and concern for one's partner."

> Recognizing the need for the relationship to be a mutual one, the Zohar comments, "One who is intimate with his wife needs to appease her with words so that she not be unimportant to him; and if he does not do this, then he should not be with her. All this in order that their wills should be as one without any mental coercion."[7]

The common thread here is that one's wife is never to be treated as an object. This could easily occur if one had constant access to his partner. Once a person treats the other as an object, the relationship quickly becomes spiritually empty and physically monotonous. This is the exact opposite of the goal.

---

5. *Shulchan Aruch, Orach Chaim* 240.

6. In his siddur, *Amudei Shamayim*. Also known as the Yaavetz, Rabbi Yaakov Emden was an eighteenth-century German scholar.

7. Rabbi Aron, *Spirituality and Intimacy* (Devora Publishing Company, 2000), p. 52.

The marital act is supposed to unite two people, not fulfill one person's agenda.

Intimacy Can Be Holy

THE EASTERN RELIGIONS EMPHASIZE the concept of shunning the material world: Everything in the material world is a necessary evil, which should be avoided when possible. These religions see the body and its needs as the enemy, conflicting with the soul's mission. Therefore the body must be controlled and restricted.

On the other extreme we have Western society, which emphasizes indulgence. Live it up with no restrictions, take advantage of all the pleasures, and pursue material wealth and fame.

What is Judaism's approach?

The Jewish concept is to find a way to unite these opposites. Judaism does not teach asceticism, but neither does it promote overindulgence. The material world is not evil. When used properly, it becomes holy. In fact, when a person focuses on serving G-d, he realizes that everything in the world was created to help us complete this objective.[8]

Food is a good example. If we eat just to fill our stomachs and satisfy our appetites because we love the taste of steak, we have "lowered" the status of the food. If we eat to have strength to live and serve G-d, we have elevated the food's status.

In short, material objects (that are permitted according to the Torah) are neither good nor bad. Man determines the moral value of our physical world based on how he uses it.

Chassidic philosophy affirms that although the body is compared to an animal, we do not need to be at odds with it. Rather

---

8. See Rambam, *Hilchot De'ot*, ch. 3.

we need to train it and gently persuade it to join forces with the soul and help it fulfill its mission.[9] This applies to every single activity, whether leisure or work, day or night.

This is also true of marital relations. We are given the task to infuse a level of meaning and holiness into this experience.

Accordingly, there are laws prescribing when a married couple may have relations. This also ensures that the couple's relationship stays vibrant, as the Torah regulates the times when relations may occur. During part of the month, the couple separates and may not be intimate.[10] Judaism also suggests that decorum be observed for the actual act. A couple should not be intimate in an exposed area, even if no one is around, for example. The expression used is "Do not be intimate where the moon can see you."[11] Even in the privacy of one's home and bedroom, there is a protocol.[12] All this is meant to bring sanctity to what could be a mere physical act for the sake of pleasure alone.

Furthermore, the Torah limits situations where people can find themselves tempted by others. Judaism prohibits a man and woman from being alone together in a room, and men and women cannot have any intimate contact unless they are married to each other. The Torah confines intimacy to a husband and wife. A person knows that any problems in his marriage must be resolved before he or she can have intimacy. This helps keep both the husband and wife more open to settling the conflicts. A home without a moral standard leaves the door open

---

9. *Kuntres U'Maayan*, ch. 6.

10. These times are connected with the woman's menstrual cycle. For a minimum of 12 days, the couple is forbidden to have relations. There are many books that detail the laws of *taharat hamishpachah*, family purity. See, for example, Rabbi Fishel Jacobs' *Family Purity* (Campus Living and Learning, 2000).

11. *Shulchan Aruch, Even HaEzer* 21.

12. See *Shulchan Aruch, Orach Chaim* 240.

for either partner to walk out and pursue pleasure elsewhere. They do not feel the need to take the necessary steps to resolve the issues.

The Jewish laws of intimacy are meant to strengthen and sanctify our marriage relationships, so that even in the midst of passion, we focus on our purpose in life — to elevate the mundane so that it becomes holy!

The Laws of Physical Intimacy Enhance the Marriage

THERE ARE A NUMBER of benefits that result from fulfilling the biblical commandments regarding marital relations properly (in addition to the main one of keeping G-d's commandments):

- ⊕ It enhances intimacy.
- ⊕ It minimizes rejection.
- ⊕ It curtails infidelity.
- ⊕ It gives the woman dignity.
- ⊕ It changes the man's perception of his wife.
- ⊕ It teaches self-control.
- ⊕ It gives offspring a head start on their spiritual journey through life.

Since many of these ideas are well known, I will be brief.

Enhances intimacy. Something that we can enjoy only occasionally is considered special and therefore generates more interest. Not only that, when the same thing is taken away from us and forbidden at some point, our interest and desire to enjoy it increases. Tell your teenager that he can't use his iPad or drive the car for two weeks. I have a feeling you won't need to wait too long to see the desire to do those very things become even more intense.

During certain times of the month, the Torah prohibits physical intimacy.[13] The Talmud concludes that "no relations are permitted for at least twelve days of the month." You can easily understand the tension (and anticipation) that will build over that time. When the couple is allowed to resume relations, they will achieve a higher level of intimacy than they could any other way.

It is quite interesting to note that when a woman is pregnant, these laws generally don't apply. How do we reconcile this continued period of availability with the notion that too much access leads to monotony? What happens to the benefits of the monthly cycle of separation and reunification?

It seems to me that the answer is quite obvious. When a woman is pregnant, she is usually not feeling herself. She may experience nausea, fatigue, anxiety, sluggishness, and other challenges. Having the couple tied to a cycle at this time would put an extra burden on the woman, so G-d, in His infinite wisdom, removed such limitations. This allows the couple to deal just with the pregnancy. It also enables the husband to provide the extra care and concern that a pregnant woman requires.

On that note I recall a woman asking me during a lecture, "What happens when the wife has passed menopause?"

Jewish law dictates that once a woman finishes her menstruation cycle, all she needs to do is go to a mikveh for one final time and then she can have relations with her husband without restrictions.

I jokingly replied, "By then, it's too late."

On a serious note, it would seem that at this stage in life when the physical desire begins to wane, it is not necessary to apply these restrictions, since the couple has matured over the years and are focusing more on the emotional part of their relationship.

---

13. Leviticus 25:18.

Minimizes rejection. Men and women are attracted to different elements of the physical union. Men are more connected to the fundamental aspect of a physical release, while women have a craving for emotional fulfillment. Given these two different modalities, it is very easy for couples to find themselves on different wavelengths.

For a woman who is seeking a sense of emotional comfort and support, her desire and interest will vary daily, depending on how she feels and what her needs are at that specific moment. For a man who is primarily interested in the physical aspect, it is much easier and quicker to be willing. This is especially true when they maintain different schedules and interests. By limiting pleasure to a specific time and set of circumstances, you are "recalibrating" the system so that both parties are on the same page.

In other words, a state of enhanced intimacy can be achieved only when both partners are willing. It can't be achieved when one person shows interest while the other doesn't. This has serious consequences for the relationship.

Here is where the rejection part comes in. One of the ways people deal with stress is to do something that gives them physical pleasure. At least temporarily, this replaces their down mood with something more enjoyable. It's quite common for people to eat when they are stressed. The physical pleasure and comfort alleviates, at least for a short time, the nasty feeling of anxiety. The same applies to all physical pleasures. One of the activities men utilize when feeling the blues is marital relations. On the other hand, when a man has a wonderful day, he often wants to celebrate by being together with his spouse in an intimate way. In the meantime, the woman may not be in sync with his moods.

The unique nature of men and the complex nature of women automatically leads to situations where either of them could feel rejected. Getting the cold shoulder or the uninterested signal makes the partner feel unwanted and unloved, and it squashes the ego. This can happen especially when each partner knows that they can be together any time. They can say, "Why do we need to be together today? It can happen tomorrow or next week."

However, when the couple has been separated for twelve days, both partners are anxious to be reunited. At the onset of the permissible time, the couple is unlikely to encounter issues of rejection. In the second half of the permissible days, they know that the time they have is limited. This, too, reduces the likelihood of rejection.

When you have a deadline, you tend to be more aware of getting things done. The same applies with intimacy.

Curtails infidelity. Infidelity is a universal plague. Many marriages are destroyed because of unfaithfulness. In many cases, it abruptly ends the marriage. Even when a relationship survives the infidelity of one of the partners, both spouses have to endure an extended amount of suffering. Once the trust between them is broken, there is a lot of hurt and pain to get through until the relationship can be reconstructed. It's questionable if it can ever be truly fixed. It certainly is difficult to go back to the way it was before.

One reason people become unfaithful is because their marital relations have become stagnant and monotonous. Since pleasure is a critical part of marriage, when it ceases to be fulfilling, the probability of cheating increases considerably.

Does this apply equally to men and women?

Based on the P's and A's theory, it would seem that men would be quicker than women to be unfaithful. When they don't achieve the pleasure they seek in the marriage, they might look elsewhere.

Women are wired to seek the A's, which means they need Affection and love. Therefore, they generally won't seek a relationship outside of their marriage unless their spouse neglects their emotional needs. In that case, they feel abandoned, but still crave to feel cared for and loved. If another person comes along and offers the assurance (or illusion) that he will fill their need, a vulnerable woman could (G-d forbid) easily become a victim.

Years ago, I met a single man in his late thirties. I asked him when he planned on getting married.

His answer threw me for a loop. "I'm worried that anyone I marry will be disloyal to me."

I assured him, "If you'll be loyal to her, she'll be loyal to you."

If a man fills his wife's emotional needs, she has no need or interest in being unfaithful, unless her husband has been disloyal himself. Then she may feel the need to take revenge or to divorce and find someone who is sincere and loyal to her.

When a couple has no limitations on their intimate relations, eventually the man may lose interest. This might tempt him to look elsewhere, and a vicious cycle ensues. The husband is dissatisfied with the marital relations, so he is less enthusiastic in filling his wife's needs. This makes her feel unloved and less interested in filling her husband's needs. The relationship deteriorates, and both are more vulnerable to being enticed by another person.

Some people might argue that, on the contrary, these laws would cause people to be unfaithful since there is a substantial period of separation time. No one says that the separation is easy; they say rather that it is worthwhile. In fact, it is because it is difficult that there is greater interest and joy when the couple is reunited. In the long run, the couple will be able to maintain satisfactory relations for many years and this reduces the temptation to look outside the marriage.

Recognizing and appreciating this reality brings us to the next topic, which is empowering the woman with dignity.

Gives the woman dignity. People don't like being pressured into doing things against their will. If I am going to do something, I need to agree to it. For that reason, Jewish law states one should never have relations with one's spouse against their will.[14] This law by extension includes not pressuring one's spouse to be intimate.

Men are typically more interested in intimacy than women.

---

14. *Shulchan Aruch, Orach Chayim*, ch. 240.

When their requests aren't met, they may apply some level of pressure. This makes a woman think that her feelings and needs are not being taken into account. This, in turn, makes her feel uncomfortable and anxious.

The Jewish laws of marriage give every woman plenty of time each month to be free from male pressure. At the same time, the emotional and physical distance between the couple creates an equal level of interest once they can resume intimacy.

Changes men's perception of their wives. Since pleasure is one of the components of a man's self-esteem, on some level his daily interaction with his wife may translate into, "This person gives me pleasure." Instead of viewing the wife as his equal, she is perceived as someone who makes him feel good. This is obviously unfortunate for a relationship. First and foremost, one's wife has many qualities and accomplishments, so why view her in terms of one particular dimension?

When a man knows that for almost two weeks he will be unable to enjoy physical interaction, he has to find some other way to have a deep relationship with his wife. In effect, he has to learn how to relate to her differently — not as a spouse, but as a friend. Seeing her this way enables him to connect to her differently when they are able to have relations once again.

> Ultimately, the Torah calls for a relationship between husband and wife which allows for the fullest expression of their love in a passionate bond. In turn, that relationship and its expression reflect a union above and an awareness which draw the couple together, not only physically and emotionally but also spiritually.[15]

This is why the Jewish laws of modesty are so essential. Although both men and women are required to dress modestly,

---

15. Aron, *Spirituality and Intimacy*, p. 121.

the laws of modesty tend to focus more on the woman. Rather than this being a burden, when a woman dresses modestly, she benefits greatly. The true worth of a person is his or her values and character. If people cherish only my appearance, they don't truly value me. The laws of modesty take the focus away from external appearance and force people to see the real person.

Likewise, if a man is esteemed because of his physical strength or his height and build, what is his true worth? The same is true of marrying someone for his money or possessions. These marriages tend to fail because there was never a commitment to marry another person — I married a car, a house, a bank account, a strong body, or a pretty person. They are all selfish, superficial considerations, and none is a good reason to keep this couple committed to each other under all circumstances.

It is so important in a marriage relationship that the husband appreciate his wife for who she is, for her inner qualities. The laws of modesty make this possible. The dress code was designed for men to look beyond the external aspect of women.

> Once, a thief walked into a heavily guarded jewelry store. After viewing the merchandise, the man scooped up a handful of gold and ran out. Immediately the guards apprehended him and he was thrown into jail. When he came to trial the judge asked the thief, "How could you be so foolish as to steal gold when there were so many people guarding this store?"
>
> "I didn't see anyone," the thief replied honestly. "All I saw was the gold."

Teaches self-control. We learned that part of our mission in this world is to control our instincts and impulses.[16] This has not only

---

16. See Chapter 11, "Make It Work, Make the Effort."

a spiritual advantage — by allowing us to connect with G-d — it also has a psychological one.

We all know the feeling of being in control. We also don't like being controlled by others. We don't want people to manipulate us. When we keep the laws that dictate when we can have marital relations, we automatically achieve a sense of inner strength. We are not slaves to our physical desires. There is a great satisfaction in saying no to an impulse.

Gives our offspring a head start. The Ba'al HaTanya teaches[17] that when parents are intimate in a holy manner, beginning with following the laws of separation and the woman immersing in a mikveh at the end of that period, and then maintaining pure and holy thoughts during marital relations, their offspring's soul descends to this world with a great spiritual sensitivity — a spiritual head start.

So we have a unique opportunity to give our children an advantage in life already from conception. What parent wouldn't be interested in giving his child a head start in life?

Physical intimacy is a foundation of a thriving marriage. The laws of relations between men and women are meant to increase the couple's feeling of fulfillment and satisfaction, and sanctify the relationship.

---

17. *Tanya*, ch. 2.

What You Can Do for Your Spouse

How to Please Your Wife

HERE'S A SIMPLE EXERCISE that will change the way you look at your relationship: Sit down and ask your wife to list five things that she would appreciate. Don't question or analyze them. Just choose two items and make them happen. Every so often repeat this exercise and you will see amazing results.

> When a woman says she will be ready in 5 minutes, it's the equivalent of a man saying he will be home in 5 minutes.

I suspect that some of those items, if not all, appear on the list below. Besides those five things, try to do as many of the suggestions that appear here. Take note of how each fulfills one or more of the three A's:

⊕ When you arrive home, greet your wife and make eye contact.

⊕ After you unwind, ask her about her day. Your questions should show that you are familiar with her plans. For example: "You had an appointment with your doctor — what did he say?"

⊕ Learn how to listen and ask questions that show you care.

- Bring your wife flowers — not only on special occasions, but even without any specific reason.
- Don't wait till Friday to ask your wife how she would like to spend the weekend. Plan in advance.
- Don't take what she does for granted — shower her with compliments.
- Respect her feelings when she becomes angry or upset.
- Offer your help, especially when your wife is tired.
- If you are late, make sure you call your wife and give a reason why you'll be late.
- If your wife's feelings are hurt, say in a sympathetic tone of voice, "I'm really sorry that you are upset," and don't say anything else. Don't give any advice and don't try to prove that it's not your fault.
- Never dismiss any of her concerns or worries as being foolish or futile.
- If your wife usually does the dishes, once in a while offer your services and do this job instead of her.
- When you are leaving the house, ask her if she needs anything. Don't forget to do everything she asks you to do.
- Embrace your wife a couple of times a day.
- Call your wife from work to ask how she is, to share some news with her, or simply to tell her, "I was thinking of you."
- Wash your wife's car.
- Show interest in her. If she is ill, inquire how she is doing.
- Show attention to your wife and don't offend her, especially in public places.
- Show respect for your wife, especially in front of the children.
- Don't oppose her in favor of the children while in their presence.
- If you are financially stable, be generous.

⊕ Give your wife small gifts like chocolates or perfumes often, and big gifts occasionally.

⊕ When your wife prepares something for dinner, make sure you praise her efforts.

⊕ If she is tired, prepare a cup of tea for her.

⊕ Find time to be together.

⊕ Tell your wife that you missed her when you were on a trip.

⊕ Buy cakes or pies that she likes.

⊕ Always say "thank you" when she does something for you.

⊕ Respect her family — don't criticize them.

⊕ When your wife talks to you, look at her; stop whatever else you might be doing. Focus all your attention on what she is saying without any distractions.

⊕ Inform your wife if you are going somewhere or if you want to rest.

⊕ Don't tell her to eat less and lose weight.

⊕ If you go somewhere, call your wife to inform her that you have arrived safely.

How to Please Your Husband

WOMEN, TOO, CAN DO the exercise I suggested for husbands above: Ask your husband to list five things that he would like you to do for him. Choose two of the five items and make them happen. In addition, I've provided you with suggestions of things your husband might like from you. Although some of these suggestions may apply more to a wife who is at home, most of these suggestions apply to all married women. As you read through these, take note of how they fulfill your husband's needs for the three P's:

⊕ Prepare yourself before your husband comes home. Try to look relaxed and not harried. After a day of work and stress, he is looking forward to a peaceful environment. He will be glad to see you looking calm and attractive.

- ⊕ Turn off your iPhone and Blackberry when he arrives and turn your attention to him.
- ⊕ Tidy up the house before he arrives home.
- ⊕ Make sure the kids are looked after and are on schedule. Stay on top of their homework and special projects.
- ⊕ When he arrives home, try not to bombard him with your troubles. Let him unwind first.
- ⊕ Dinner should be ready before he comes home from work. Even if he comes back late, have dinner waiting for him.
- ⊕ Don't complain if he is late for dinner. You can talk about this issue at a different time.
- ⊕ Try not to schedule activities where you have to go out at night while he is home.
- ⊕ Keep him company while he is eating (even if he comes home late).
- ⊕ Be considerate with the finances.
- ⊕ Don't attack or criticize him. Use other approaches to communicate a complaint.[1]
- ⊕ Don't convey messages that make him feel he is a failure.
- ⊕ Don't be overly persistent, even when dealing with important issues. Broach them with gentleness.
- ⊕ Boost his ego: Tell him how much admiration you have for him as a husband, father, provider, and human being.
- ⊕ Give him time for his hobbies or social life.
- ⊕ Show interest in intimacy. He should perceive that this is a mutual interest.

---

1. See Chapter 18, "Step 2: It's Not What You Say, but How You Say It."

- Don't slight him in the presence of others.
- Don't oppose him in favor of the children while in their presence.
- Respect his family. If you have problems with them, it might be better to avoid this topic.
- When he speaks to you, focus all your attention on what he is saying without any distractions.
- Inform him if you are going somewhere or if you want to rest.
- Don't tell him to eat less or lose weight.
- If you go somewhere, call and inform him that you have arrived safely.

Keep in mind what you can do to please your spouse.

Glossary

ASHKENAZI: Jews who originate from Europe

BAR MITZVAH: When a Jewish boy becomes 13 and is obligated to perform the commandments

BAT MITZVAH: When a Jewish girl becomes 12 and is obligated to perform the commandments

BILAAM: Gentile prophet who tried to curse the Jews

CHABAD HOUSE: Jewish center to promote Jewish observance

CHASSID (pl. CHASSIDIM): Orthodox Jew who follows a Rebbe

GEMARA: Explanation of the Mishnah

KIPA: Skullcap that Jewish men wear

MEZUZAH: Small parchment with Torah passages, affixed to the doorpost of Jewish homes

MIKVEH: Ritual bath

MISHNAH: The first section of the Talmud, compiled circa 200 CE

MITZVAH: A commandment

PESACH: The Passover holiday

PIRKEI AVOT: Ethics of our fathers (part of the Mishnah)

ROSH YESHIVAH: Dean of Jewish learning academy

SEDER: Festive meal commemorating the Exodus, held on the first night or first two nights of Passover

SEPHARDI: Jews who originate from Spain and Middle Eastern countries

SHIVAH: Seven-day mourning period

SHULCHAN ARUCH: Code of Jewish law

TORAH: The Bible (also includes other Jewish texts)

YESHIVAH: Learning academy for Jewish studies